COURAGE TO BE
real

LETTING THE REAL YOU SHINE THROUGH

SUSAN M. AUSTIN, M.D.

Scripture quotations taken from the Amplified® Bible are marked AMP. Copyright © 1954, 1958, 1962, 1964, 1965, 1987 by The Lockman Foundation. La Habra, CA. Used by permission.

Scripture quotations taken from the Common English Bible are marked CEB. Copyright © 2011 by Common English Bible. Retrieved from http://www.commonenglishbible.com.

Scripture quotations taken from the English Standard Version are marked ESV. Copyright © 2001 by Crossway Bibles, a division of Good News Publishers. Used by permission. All rights reserved.

Scripture quotations taken from the King James Version of the Bible® are marked KJV. Copyright © 1982 by Broadman & Holman Publishers, Nashville, TN. Used by permission. All rights reserved.

Scripture quotations taken from the New American Standard Bible® are marked NASB. Copyright © 1960, 1962, 1963, 1968, 1971, 1972, 1973, 1975, 1977, 1995 by The Lockman Foundation. Used by permission.

Scripture quotations taken from the HOLY BIBLE, NEW INTERNATIONAL VERSION® are marked NIV. Copyright © 1973, 1978, 1984 Biblica. Used by permission of Zondervan. All rights reserved.

Scripture quotations taken from the New King James Version of the Bible are marked NKJV. Copyright © 1982 by Thomas Nelson, Inc. Used by permission. All rights reserved.

Scripture quotations taken from the Holy Bible, New Living Translation are marked NLT. Copyright 1996, 2004. Used by permission of Tyndale House Publishers, Inc., Wheaton, Illinois 60189. All rights reserved.

Scripture quotations taken from the Revised Standard Version of the Bible are marked RSV, copyright © 1946, 1952, and 1971 the Division of Christian Education of the National Council of the Churches of Christ in the United States of America. Used by permission. All rights reserved.

To contact the author:

www.couragetobereal.com
www.inward-bound-adventures.net

Dedication

I dedicate this book to all of the people who have graciously allowed me to work with and counsel them, who have opened their hearts in the deepest of wounded places, and allowed God's healing light to shine into the darkness.

Praise for Courage to Be Real

"Susan Austin has bravely beckoned the real self to come out of hiding and step into the light. She coaxes our false self to lay down its defenses and to allow our real self to come forth and experience all the glory and majesty we were created to enjoy.

Courage to Be Real is artfully written, lovely to comprehend, and easy to apply practically. You will recognize yourself in its pages and be energized to let the real you shine through!"

—WENDY K. WALTERS
Motivational Speaker, Author of *Intentionality: Live on Purpose!*
www.wendykwalters.com

"*Courage to Be Real* is one of the greatest treasures ever released by a physician to bring healing and wholeness to the masses. An important need in our culture and mankind in general is healing broken hearts. Dr. Susan Austin's teaching and stories are practical, leading to increased self awareness. Applying what she teaches helps you be an overcomer, realize your potential, and live your big dreams.

As Dr. Susan says, 'This book is about what it takes to become the real and best person you were created to be.' Enjoy!"

—JOSEPH PECK, M.D.
The Time Doctor, Author of *I Was Busy, Now I'm Not*
www.empower2000.com

"*Courage to Be Real* offers an amazing view of who I really am. There are many and wildly different ways of seeing ourselves. Dr. Austin has taken some of the most far reaching views from the Sandfords, Arthur Burk, Mark Virkler, Daniel Siegel, James Masterson and the Life Model and provided a smoothly flowing narrative that could take each of us the rest of our lives to explore. Any of these sources alone are enough to bend one's mind but together would be confusing and overwhelming. Yet because each source is woven through the life and identity of Dr. Austin's own experiences the reader will only find refreshing streams of life and gently climbing paths to recovering and discovering our true selves.

—E. JAMES WILDER, PH.D.
Author, International Speaker, Developer of the Life Model

"Don't be fooled by the size of this little book! It is filled with great nuggets of wisdom and insight, gleaned from years of study, reflection, and Susan's own practice. I have known Susan for many years, so I feel confident to say she has a special gift for integrating the benefits of many different practitioners and theorists' contributions. And now she is offering this to the rest of us! Even so, it is written to be understood by all—lay persons and therapists alike. I have learned so much from her compassionate, creative and caring insights, which have helped me on my personal journey. It is Susan's desire to honor God in all that she does, and I believe He is pleased with the results. I encourage you to read it and apply it to your own life. It will change the way you see yourself, others, and life! God bless you on your journey of discovering more of who God made you to be.

—ANNETTE McTIERNAN, LMHC
Schenectady N.Y. Outpatient Medical Health Clinic

"You will recognize yourself in these pages and be gently encouraged, inspired, and equipped to allow yourself to become a better version of you—who you really are!

"*Courage to Be Real* is written from Susan Austin's heart to your heart with love. Dare to embark on a journey of self-discovery and step out of the shadows into God's glorious light. The best is yet to come."

—LYNNE LEE
Christian Life Coach, Life Coach Trainer, Author of *How to Hear God*
www.ChristianLifeCoaching.co.uk

"*Courage to Be Real* reminds us of God's desire for each one of us to become the wonderful, unique person He created. The book provides a road map. The essential direction in the road map is encountering love—God. God gives us people for the journey, intellect to reflect, pray, imagine and understand God's love for each of us. We can be healed, transformed, and fulfilled. Therefore we can be a gift to others on the journey."

—JOSEPH BYRNES, LMSW
Program Administrator, Children with Special Needs
Westchester County Department of Health

"Susan does a wonderful job of weaving scriptural truths together with sound clinical observations. The result is a book packed with insight, encouragement and practical tools for those seeking wholeness."

—PETE CAFARCHIO.
Professional Coach
www.petecoaching.com

Contents

Appendix

Opening

"You are all children of the light and children of the day. We do not belong to the night or to the darkness."

1 THESSALONIANS 5:5, NLT

INTRODUCTION

Awakening to Your Real Self

You are a masterpiece—literally. You are a piece of exquisite workmanship fashioned by the Master Creator! This life you are living is important. You are a treasure. You have a unique purpose, and a destiny that is yours and yours alone. You are an unfolding miracle. You are in the process of becoming you ... the real you!

I bless your heart to awaken more and more to the purposes and design for which you were created. I bless your eyes to see yourself the way God created you to be. I bless your ears to hear what your Creator says about you as you embrace the extraordinary adventure which is your life. I bless you with courage to tackle every problem, to be unflinching in your ability to acknowledge, explore, and find solutions to the painful circumstances of your life. I bless your heart to dream, to hope, to desire, and to expect. I bless you to love truth with all of your heart, and to see beyond the horizon into the magnificent moment of now—the place where you have choices!

Just as there is a key to every lock, every problem has a solution. Every difficulty you encounter presents you with a doorway into your destiny. The gifts are there, inside you. You already have all that you need within you to accomplish your purpose and to fulfill the dreams of your heart. Now is the time to step forward into the treasure hunt of discovering you. It is time to seek and to become and to cherish your real self!

Becoming Your Best Self

This book is about what it takes to become the real and best person you were created to be. It is a true account written from my personal experience. I am a psychiatrist who has worked with hurting people in individual counseling for the past 25 years, and I am also a person who has tackled my own painful healing process. I have learned so much about what it takes to become whole and to be real. It is not a quick fix, but a journey and a process. No matter where you are on your path, there are things you can learn and choices you can make that will help you realize your great potential.

Overview

First, I describe the core self—the real self—and the journey of becoming all that we were created to be. Then I share some of my own story. I describe the problems: the variety of hurtful experiences we can go through. I talk about the different types of wounds and traumas. Since abandonment is such a commonplace and painful experience, I go into some detail about it. I describe the struggle that a sensitive person goes through, being more likely to be on the receiving end of the hurtful reactions of others.

I explain what defenses are: the counterproductive ways in which we try to keep from being overwhelmed by emotional pain. Anger is addressed as both a major defense, and as a suppressed emotion, and I look at the difference between the two. I also go into some detail about Codependency, which I have found to be an extremely common and destructive pattern of defensive behavior. I talk about how we learn to identify with people who treat us abusively, internalize it, and often treat ourselves in the same ways.

I believe that we are here to find the solutions to these problems, so in the next part we look at some of these solutions. I discuss the importance of being honest emotionally. In the chapter, Jesus Our Healer, I describe my personal experience with Jesus as the One who deeply desires to heal our hearts. I also look at the challenges we face in believing this, and in being able to receive that healing. I include a chapter on the difference between our spirit and our soul. I share some of the stories I have witnessed of people who have been healed, and talk about the importance of rekindling the dreams of your heart.

Lastly, there is a section providing tools which are helpful in the recovery process. Among these are the ability to quiet your mind, journaling, play, joyful relationships, eating healthy, exercise, and declaring who you are as God sees you. I even include some of my favorite jokes!

Resources

At the end of the book I list a number of resources that I have found helpful in the recovery process.

About three years ago I established Inward Bound Adventures (*www.inward-bound-adventues.net*), a foundation for me to be able to share many of these concepts. Since that time, I have been facilitating webinars, seminars and small group experiences (6–15 people) where we incorporate these topics into creative group exercises. The seminars are designed to provide practical tools and takeaway skills which assist people in the process of being authentic, finding healing, and becoming the joyful, creative, and productive individuals we were created to be.

Take your time reading this book. As some of these ideas touch upon your own experiences, give yourself the opportunity to mull them over. Talk to a friend or counselor about what you are feeling. Journal, if that is something you enjoy doing. This is a book about the process of healing and becoming real. Honor your own process and stay with it. *Thar's gold in them thar hills!*

1
CHAPTER ONE

The Core Self

---

*The core self is the unique, individual spark
of God's own life designated to be you!*

When I speak of becoming real, I am talking about your core self developing into the magnificence of the being that your Creator has always had in mind for you. This core self is your spirit sent forth into a physical body, with the potential of a developing soul. The core self is the true you, designed to grow in love. As it emerges, the core self can be wounded, abandoned, or crushed. If there are not loving, nurturing people to care for it, the core self will hide, shrivel, and in many cases, go to sleep and not participate in life.

When that happens, the child will develop a false self to live life, although in reality, this is only existing, not really living as we were designed to live. At the time when a wound occurs, a child can get stuck in a specific area of development and not progress. A child cannot mature in healthy ways without the ongoing support, love, wisdom, encouragement, and direction of healthy adults. When we get stuck, our core self has not had the help it needs to be able to manage the particular developmental challenges that need to be mastered.

This is always a painful state of affairs. Most of the time we don't know we are wounded or stuck. We don't have the concepts or the words to even begin to describe what has happened to us. We are simply living life from a false self, which includes the various addictions, isolation, recurrent anger, controlling behavior, codependency, lack of spontaneity and creativity, living below your potential, etc. This is not what we were created for!

> *When the core self has been crushed or abandoned or wounded, and is in hiding or asleep, that self will need help!*

When the core self has been crushed or abandoned or wounded, and is in hiding or asleep, that self will need help! It will be painful for the core self to awaken. The same trauma that caused us to go into hiding will have to be faced and worked through in order for a person to become real. There are developmental delays which must be corrected.

We are all wounded and living false to some degree. Our Creator knows this and is, I believe, in the active process of calling each of us to the healing and activation of our true core self.

So, yes, it is a painful journey to become real. But that's okay. We are up to the challenge. We were created with all that we need to go through this process and to come out being magnificent! We need to help each other! Each of us has a gift to give. Each of us has something that the rest of us need in order to be the beautiful, outstanding, wonderful creation that we are designed to be.

The Bible says:

> "... put off your old self (false self), which belongs to your former (broken human) manner of life and is corrupt (damaged) through deceitful desires (defenses), and be renewed in the spirit of your mind (awakened), and put on the the new self (core self), created after the likeness of God in true righteousness and holiness."
>
> —EPHESIANS 4:22-24 ESV *(paraphrase and parenthesis added)*

CHAPTER TWO

Finding My Way

They told me in medical school that I would make a good psychiatrist, but I wanted to be a "real" doctor. Make that, my father wanted me to be a "real" doctor. I had no idea that my choices were made to please him. I thought becoming a doctor was what I wanted—never mind that I *hated* medical school. It felt so tedious to sit through hour upon hour of lectures with every instructor talking in a language that felt foreign to me. I wondered why everything had to be said in "medicalese." To me it just seemed like a way to keep people from understanding what the doctors were talking about.

During my medical training, I chafed at having to have a reference to the medical literature in order to be able to give an opinion. If an idea or treatment had not been "proven" through scientific testing, it was considered invalid to even discuss it. Because my strengths were much more in the realm of intuition and emotional understanding, I found it difficult to converse with many of the other doctors, who were predominantly logically and rationally oriented. At that time I did not have the language to help me understand what I was feeling.

At one point the Dean of my medical school called me into his office to have a talk about why I was having a hard time. I expected that he might be planning on kicking me out of medical school, but quite the opposite happened. He told me that some doctors have a harder time dealing with all the pain and suffering and death … and that I needed to take that into consideration as I went through my training. It was the first time someone had helped me understand that I was a highly sensitive person. Even more significant, he helped me understand that being sensitive was a valid way to be.

Throughout my career in general medicine, I tried hard to fit in, to do it right. I became a family physician and spent three long years in the Public Health Service in South Dakota. At times I was the only M.D. in three counties of potential tractor accidents. There were times when I was solo in full charge of a clinic, emergency room, small nursing home, and 28-bed hospital. I delivered babies during snowstorms with no obstetrician for 60 miles. I felt continually overwhelmed. I always wanted to talk more with my patients. To me it seemed like their bottled-up emotions were contributing greatly to their medical problems, but there was never time to really talk—to get to the bottom of things. There was little room for reflection or exploration of feelings. It took ten years for me to realize: "I don't like this. I'm not good at it. I don't want to do this anymore."

So I stopped. I didn't know what I was looking for. I thought there was something wrong with me. I had tried really hard to be a good doctor. I felt like a whipped dog. It was discouraging after having spent so much time, effort, and money on something that just didn't work for me. I didn't know how to process what I was going through.

I didn't have the words or concepts to help me understand what was happening. I didn't realize that I was going through a growth process, I just thought I was a failure.

My mom talked me into trying psychiatry, a big step for her, because in my growing up years, no one ever went to a psychiatrist. It wasn't done. Psychiatry was not considered to be a valid field of study. If you saw a psychiatrist, it meant that there was something terribly wrong with you. In our home we never talked about the real problems that existed. It wasn't until I began studying psychiatry that I started to realize that I had come from a highly wounded family.

I entered a Psychiatry Residency Training Program, and from the start I knew it was something I liked, something I could do. They were right about me in medical school—I was good at psychiatry! I enjoyed talking with people, listening, helping them make sense of their struggles, and having time to connect.

What makes someone spend ten years doing something they don't like, something that doesn't fit their gifts and talents? In my case, my particular set of talents was not recognized as legitimate in my home or the community where I grew up. I was sensitive, imaginative, creative, and adventuresome with a pioneer spirit. But my environment was quite rigid, conformist, authoritarian, and punitive. You didn't question, you obeyed. Distressing feelings were not discussed. I didn't know that my family was troubled. We never talked about things that were frightening or painful. I never realized that my father was an alcoholic or that my parents' fights were deeply disturbing to my sister, my brother, and me. We fit the profile of a dysfunctional family: "don't talk, don't feel, don't trust." Sadly, many of my friends grew up in similar environments. We just thought it was normal.

I didn't know that I wasn't being real, wasn't expressing the true feelings in my heart. I didn't know who I was, I just tried to get by. I did the right things. Getting good grades in school was highly valued in my family, so I got good grades. I kept going and I didn't think much about it. I didn't know how. I had no words for what I felt and no role models to follow, and therefore, could not process the feelings. You can't think things through if you don't have the words. And you can't think things through without someone to talk them over with. I didn't know anyone who could help me understand myself. That's how I ended up spending ten years trying to be someone who wasn't me.

> *I didn't know who I was, I just tried to get by. I had no words for what I felt and no role models to follow.*

Food was a comfort. It became a lifelong addiction. Food became tied into fear for me very early in life. Eventually, I got into some pretty severe addictions, food and cigarettes among the most acceptable. I didn't know that I was medicating my pain. I didn't even know that I was in pain. I didn't realize I was numbing myself, shutting down, and becoming less and less my real self. The summer that I was 16 I returned to camp in the mountains. That's when I noticed that the lights had gone out. Nature once had had a glorious effect upon my heart, but I couldn't see the splendor anymore. Mechanical sex had dampened my spirit, which could no longer see beauty. I knew something was wrong, but didn't know what. Again, I had no one to talk to about it. I had no words to be able to think it through.

My mom was a wonderful person. She and my sister, similar in personality, were lifelong friends. Me? Nobody's fault, but she didn't "get" me. I was a feeler, she was a thinker. She said I was "sentimental" as a child. I cried frequently, and still do. I never saw my mother cry. She found it difficult to understand me and was therefore poorly able to help me process my emotions or to develop my abilities. The psychological term is *abandonment*. It is summed up in the phrase, "children should be seen and not heard." But what if no one really sees you? Sees who you are. What you like. What you're good at. What you need help with. What if they see you only through their own lenses of what you should be like? We grow and develop only as we are seen, mirrored, nurtured and celebrated. That's how we come to know ourselves. Only in relationship. Only with help.

Eventually I got help, and lots of it. Adult Children of Alcoholics, psychotherapy, growth workshops, trainings, conferences. I am very grateful to all of the people who have helped me in my recovery process. They have taught me so much about what it means to be real and how to get there. I have had wonderful mentors and teachers, among them:

- Dr. Tom Hawkins, who taught me about what it means to have a divided heart and how to heal;

- Dr. Edward Smith, who taught me how to pray for people to receive God's healing presence instead of just counseling them;

- Arthur Burk, who taught me, among other things, the difference between the human spirit and the soul, and how to encourage my spirit to take the lead;

- Dr. Jim Wilder and the Thrive Team, who taught me how our brain is designed to function and to heal, through joyful relationships, and how to help myself and others through the Immanuel (God with us) Process;

- Dr. James Masterson, who continues to teach me through his book, *The Search for the Real Self*;

- Dr. Irene Cirillo, who has been my therapist for the past six years, and who convinced me that anger was not keeping me safe. She taught me to be flexible, to love myself, and to come to Jesus for all the help I need;

- Dr. Lance Wallnau who encouraged me to find the purpose for which I was created and to go for it;

- Wendy Walters, my first coach, who believed that Inward Bound Adventures was a dream destined to come true, and who lovingly walked me through my first tottering steps in that direction;

- Pete Cafarchio, who was my business coach during the year that this book was written, and whose gentle and wise counsel has been invaluable;

- and my friend and prayer partner, Annette McTiernan, who has shared the adventure of learning all these things with me over the past 25 years.

So now I share with you what I have learned. Our lives have value. You too are a treasure. You have a purpose and a destiny that is special and unique. There is no one else like you. There is no one with your particular gifts and talents. No one who can do what you were created to do. It is through the process of acknowledging and addressing our struggles that we become real. God wants us to be real with Him, to tell Him our needs and our feelings, confide in Him about our struggles, and ask Him all of our questions.

It's time to awaken and to catch hold of the mystery and adventure that awaits you. I can tell you that it is worth the struggle. If you have breath in your body, even if you are dying, you have a purpose. More purpose! The real you is alive at the very core of your being! Your Creator knows where you are and who you are. He knows that you are one-of-a-kind, He loves you endlessly, and is committed to your healing and your joy. I bless your spirit to awaken to the destiny and purpose and delight that is your heritage as a child of God.

*You have a
purpose and
a destiny that
is special and
unique. There
is no one else
like you.*

Problems

"The Lord is close to the brokenhearted and saves those who are crushed in spirit."

PSALM 34:18, NIV

CHAPTER THREE

The Wounds

There is room in the halls of pleasure
For a long and lordly train,
But one by one we must all file on
Through the narrow aisles of pain.

FROM "SOLITUDE" BY ELLA WHEELER WILCOX

We are all wounded. We are all searching for healing, wholeness, restoration, recovery. Is healing possible? Is there really hope for becoming whole? Is it possible to become well, excellent, magnificent?

At the age of four, Jamie had been brutally molested by a neighborhood boy. Her mother, probably the victim of abuse herself, had been unable to help Jamie understand what had happened to her, or to help her recover from the trauma. Jamie had nothing but a vague sense that something bad had happened to her as a child. She had no memory of details. As an adult, she stayed away from any close relationships with men, and became highly anxious if a man approached her in a way that suggested romantic interest. As we worked together to explore and put words to her feelings and memories, the true story of the abuse gradually became clear. Jamie has been able to feel, tolerate, understand, and ultimately embrace the wounded little girl part of her. This gave her the ability for the first time to consider a real romantic relationship.

Trauma happens when you go through something overwhelming as a child and you go through it alone, with no one there to help you process it. If, as a child, you go through something overwhelming, but have a caring individual to help you sort out and process what you went through, the event does not have to become a trauma.

When an experience does not get processed, it continues to exist as a triggerable bundle of raw emotion in the brain.

Once processed it gets filed in the brain's library as an experience. If the event is not processed, it becomes a trauma. When an experience does not get filed (i.e. becomes a trauma), it continues to exist as a triggerable bundle of raw emotion in the brain. It's like a neon sign inside that starts flashing whenever a similar experience reminds your brain of what happened to you. The feelings rush to the surface with all the intensity of the original trauma. We call this "being triggered" or "having our buttons pushed." It is automatic and involuntary, and it happens to all of us. Sometimes the trigger is not noticeably similar to the original trauma, yet somehow our brain connects it with the trauma, and we react as if we are that overwhelmed child again.

The only way our human brains are able to process overwhelming emotions is when someone helps us. We need the help of another person to be able to put words to what we are feeling, to tolerate the feelings, to understand what is happening to us, and to receive comfort and consolation. When this happens we can remain ourselves, and know who we are. We can understand what has happened and come to feel good about ourselves, even if we have gone through a tremendously painful situation. If we do not get the help we need, the emotions do not get processed. Instead they become locked inside.

It's as if you have a child in a dark box sealed inside of you—trapped and in pain, feeling fear and confusion, feeling helpless and hopeless. Because these feelings are too painful to deal with alone, our brains automatically shut them away, locking them inside. Then we live with a divided heart: one part of our "self" locked inside with overwhelming emotions, and another part of our "self" living as if those emotions do not exist. The part that is locked inside does not grow and develop, because the way that we grow and develop is by experience. So that part remains "childlike" in it's way of perceiving and relating. There is not actually a child inside. This is a way of referring to the brain's immature way of processing emotional information, referring to this as the "inner child". Experientially, it is very much like having an actual child living inside of you.

The part of us that is living as if those emotions do not exist (the denial part or false self) automatically "hates" the part that is holding the overwhelming emotions. Why? Because that part has had no way to process or understand themselves within this experience. There is no way for that part to feel "good" about themselves. Feeling good means "I am loved and accepted." A trauma suffered alone does not allow me to feel loved or accepted, therefore, I feel "bad". Bad means "I am not loved. I am not welcomed. I am not connected." In a way, "bad" means that I am less than human. This emotional dividedness is part of our human condition, and requires help in understanding the emotions, help in being able to tolerate the overwhelming feelings, and help in resolving them. This help only comes from being loved. In other words, **we need to know that we are not alone.**

Whatever experiences we go through as a child create our beliefs. And whatever we believe causes us to have feelings. This is true for both positive and negative experiences. It looks like this:

Experience > Belief > Feeling

For example:

- ✒ **Experience:** Your art teacher in grade school was critical or belittling of your drawings.

- ✒ **Belief:** You believe you are a terrible artist.

- ✒ **Feeling:** Later on if anyone asks you to draw something you may automatically start feeling dejected and insecure.

The *feeling* tells you that you are *believing* something bad about yourself, and the *belief* comes from what you have *experienced*.

So when you have a feeling (especially recurrent patterns of troubling feelings), you can generally trace it back to a belief. And that belief will have come from an experience. It has been said that most of our beliefs about ourselves and others are well in place by the time we reach the age of 18 months!

Types of Wounds

There are two types of wounds or traumas:

- ❧ Type __A__ Traumas come from the __A__bsence of the good and necessary experiences we need as a child. These Type A Traumas cause the "abandonment" wounds.

- ❧ Type __B__ Traumas are the __B__ad things which happen, such as physical, verbal, or sexual abuse.

Both Type A and Type B Traumas involve having overwhelming emotions.

Type A Trauma is, in my opinion, the worst. It stems from the absence of the good things we need in order to grow and develop in a healthy way. We are designed to learn trust and security from a safe, stable, nurturing relationship with our mother (or other primary caretaker).

Type A Wounds

Rose's mom was a busy doctor. She was delighted to have had her first child, but the demands of her job were many. She had no real understanding of her daughter's attachment needs or the importance of secure connection, especially during the first few years of life. Rose had numerous caretakers. She did not have consistent connection with any one person during her early formative years. This set the stage for a poorly developed sense of self, or what is sometimes referred to as a fragile ego.

The first months of life are a time of building security. This security comes from being fed and held, loved and responded to in a predictable and consistent manner. It is important that there be one person, usually the mother, who builds a secure foundation for interpersonal relationship with the child. This consistency of connection with one person is the foundation for building a secure relational identity for the rest of one's life.

Security is built as a child is fed and held, loved and responded to in a predictable and consistent manner.

We learn joy as we connect with mommy through eye contact and pleasurable interactions. We discover the joy of being with someone who loves being with us. We learn that mommy is sensitive to our feelings and needs. She knows when we have had enough and need to rest. We learn that our boundaries are respected. As a developing infant we are designed to flow with our mother in cycles of joy and rest.

A healthy mom also teaches us how to return to joy from all the difficult emotions. She does this by sharing those emotions with us, understanding, putting words to feelings, and showing us the pathway back to joy and a sense of being loved.

An illustration of this would be when a mom comes in and finds her child with a dirty diaper and at first wrinkles her nose at the smell. The child notices mom's disapproval and starts to whimper. Mom immediately notices the child's distress and says, "Ooh, that's a yucky smell, but I love you so much, see, we're going to get you changed and all nice and clean!" bringing the child into an experience of comfort and joy.

As first our eyes and then our muscles develop, we receive from mommy the encouragement to explore. A healthy mother will support the child's growing capacity for investigation of the world and new relationships. She will provide a secure place of refuge and comfort for the child to return to when his or her explorations become too challenging. And she will continue to provide both the encouragement to explore and a safe haven for rest as her little one goes through the back and forth process of developing his or her own separate self.

These are the good and necessary things that we all need, and the absence of these experiences is a Type A Trauma.

If the mother does not have a healthy self, she cannot nurture a healthy sense of self in her child. There are many points at which this can be a problem. There may be a lack of basic security. Or, the mom may cling to the child as a way to try to be loved herself. She may engulf the child with her own unmet needs. If it threatens her own shaky self-image, a wounded mother may not be able to encourage the child's exploration and growth. She may reward the child for clinging to her, and reject the child emotionally if the child makes an effort to explore his or her own world separately from the mother. She may not even be aware that she is doing this, but this leaves the child with an "abandoned self," a self which will tend to stay locked up inside, because we each need encouragement to become our real self!

In a healthy situation, as we grow and develop, our mother will mirror and reassure us in our own unique personality, our likes and dislikes, the things we enjoy doing. She encourages us to explore and welcomes us back into her secure embrace when we need security and comfort. This happens over and over as we learn to become a separate self, our own person.

If, for whatever reason, these processes do not happen, or happen in an inadequate or limited way, it leads to Type A Traumas or wounds of the "self." The "real self," which is wounded or undeveloped, is unable (or poorly able) to meet the challenges of life, and remains in a sense, locked up. The child will develop a "false self," ways of relating that are not expressions of the heart or the real self, but are instead ways of trying to cope with the abandonment trauma.

> *When the "real self" is wounded or undeveloped, it will have trouble meeting the challenges of life.*

Teddy was a gentle, quiet little boy who had a gift of being sensitive to the feelings of others. His mom was a quite needy, extroverted woman who tended to cover up her own feelings by being highly talkative, dramatic and overly involved in big projects. She had difficulty relating to her small son's delicate emotions and was essentially unable to help him understand and manage his feelings. Teddy became something of a loner, preferring to be by himself, and had a poorly developed capacity to tolerate his own emotions or to understand the emotions of others.

Typical of the false self are tendencies to be preoccupied with being perfect, or needing to act in certain ways in order to feel acceptable. Examples of the false self include having to be busy all the time, always having to "do the right thing," being chronically anxious about the choices you make, isolating, being a clown, obsessive neatness, chronic anger, addictions, bullying others, worrying about how you look, being critical, and being afraid to take risks. These are painful and pervasive patterns. There are many variations on this theme. One of the most common is to have an "abandoned self," with a weak or absent sense of identity, and a tendency to cling to others for a feeling of worth. Another is an "engulfed self," one in which your boundaries have not been respected, with the result of believing that you have to avoid relationships in order to be safe.

Type B Wounds

Type B Traumas are the "Bad" things that happen to us. Sally was molested by a man in a yellow raincoat at age three. There was no one to help her process and come to terms with this. As an adult she has an aversion to the color yellow, but no understanding of why this might be true.

Type B traumas are extensive in our society. It is estimated that one out of every three girls will be sexually abused before the age of 16, and the frequency is only slightly less for boys. Our culture has become more aware that physical abuse is wrong (and reportable). When I was growing up, physical abuse was, for the most part, accepted as normal and not discussed. Even today, however, it is generally considered understandable that sometimes parents "lose it" and hit their kids. Emotional abuse is even more rampant. Harsh, cruel words can become arrows that deeply pierce our hearts. If a child has a trusted person to help them understand the abuse and work through their emotions, these experiences do not have to result in trauma.

When the pain of a Type B Trauma reaches a certain level, the mind will split off the pain from the rest of your personality. You may notice that you act in certain ways most of the time, but that every once in a while, you get triggered and act in ways that are distressing to you. When you follow the path of those triggered behaviors, you will likely come to a wounded area or trauma. The distressing emotions may be partially or completely walled off from the rest of your identity. When we do this work and go to the places that are painful, I have often heard people say, "I must be making this up." As the beliefs or emotions or memories become conscious, it can feel like what you are sensing inside is "not you." It can be quite unsettling at first to become acquainted with a part of yourself that is holding the feelings from an traumatic incident.

We all have many Type A and Type B Traumas. It is through the acknowledgement, honest expression, and sharing of the feelings and fears with trusted others and with God, that we travel the road to recovery. It takes courage to be real. And you have that courage inside of you. It is part of your birthright!

Wherever you are wounded, it is there that you have a gift. If you have been terrified, you are designed to be fearless. If you have experienced great sadness, you have the gift of being a joy-giver. What's important is to acknowledge the wound and to search for the cure. Search and keep searching until you find the gifts that are within you. Your life is intended to be satisfying and delightful. Don't settle for anything less. You have it within you to be awesome. The greater the wound, the greater the gifting.

You are designed to wrestle with the traumas that have happened to you and to find release. It is in acknowledging and addressing our wounds that we develop our gifts and become all that we were created to be. Our spirits are marvelously resilient. You are a unique treasure. You've got what it takes. I invite you:

To Dream the Impossible Dream
To Fight the Unbeatable Foe
To Bear with Unbearable Sorrow
To Run where the Brave dare not Go

CHAPTER FOUR

Abandonment

I n the last chapter we discussed Type A Trauma—trauma which results from one of the most painful wounds, abandonment. When we have not been mothered adequately, we develop feelings of abandonment. This often manifests as a fear of being alone. Whether your mother was ill, absent, too busy, or emotionally wounded herself, or if you did not have a mother (or other mothering person) to consistently nurture you and to mirror you as an infant and young child, your "real self" became abandoned. This is a Type A Trauma: the absence of the good things you need in order to grow and develop in a healthy way.

Without healthy, dependable love and encouragement you cannot grow and become your true self. In any area in which you are not seen, nurtured, encouraged and applauded, it's as though your spirit—that spark of life that is you—shrivels up and lies down as if it is dead. It's as if our real self goes into a dark cave and just exists there in silence and an aching solitude. This aching aloneness is what we call depression. We try to medicate it away with alcohol, gambling, entertainment, or even shopping. But the experience of depression is really the abandoned self coming into awareness. It is exquisitely painful. It is a signal, an internal cry for help. It is the real self in the anguish of abandonment, groaning for real relationship, real nurturing, real love. When a person struggles with depression, there is most likely an abandoned real self.

When the real self has been abandoned, a child (in their human personality or soul) will look outside of themselves to try to figure out what is normal. We try to find acceptance and belonging by being like other people. We struggle to look good, to do the acceptable thing, to talk well, to be a fun person. The problem with all of this is that if it comes from a "false self," it is really a desperate attempt to get away from the real self inside which is abandoned. The false self is engaged in a never-ending quest for security, a black hole: "looking for love in all the wrong places."

> *The false self is engaged in a never-ending quest for security, a black hole: "looking for love in all the wrong places."*

One of my clients told me, "I put pressure on myself to be sexy, cool, passionate, interesting. My mom was into excitement. I feel like I should be doing exciting things now. Spending time with myself? I don't want to do that. I want to do things that count. It only counts if I do something important. It only counts if I have a story to tell about how wonderful my life is. It's always about what's the next thing to do. How do I make myself useful? It's only what I do or how I look. I feel so sad ... so needy ... so empty. I want a formula. How do I just 'be?'"

The false self is extremely strong. It is the part of our personality that is dead set against ever acknowledging that abandoned, needy, empty "self." The false self is a survival mechanism, and I'm pretty sure we all have one! Not one of us has been unconditionally loved, even if we had the very best of parents. Whether it's parental woundedness, illness, fatigue, loss or accident, children will at some point experience difficult emotions without the help of a parent to process them. It is impossible for a child to handle or understand or connect to what they are feeling without a caring, safe, and emotionally mature adult to help. The child's heart literally goes into hiding, and a false self emerges to try to handle life.

The false self engages in all sorts of activities and undertakings in order to try to feel important, accepted, valued and loved—from marrying a "strong" individual, to becoming a highly sought-after (and usually extremely busy) professional. Some people try to find a sense of self worth through their children. A mother who has an abandoned self will sometimes cling to her child in an effort to feel loved and accepted. When this happens the child's true self will be abandoned because the mother is not relating to the child as a separate and unique individual, but is trying to find a sense of self through the love that she receives from her child. In this way, the experience of an abandoned self is passed from generation to generation.

There are literally hundreds of ways that the false self tries to keep the real feelings of abandonment and aloneness from coming into conscious awareness. Some of the most common are addictions, busyness, co-dependency, anger, isolation, controlling behaviors, people-pleasing, self-injury, perfectionism, numbing, avoidance of people, obsessing, being critical, staying in abusive relationships ... the list goes on and on. Frequently the unacknowledged real feelings are expressed through the physical body when the true self is not able to handle them. Many physical ailments have their root in emotions that one has never had words to express, or a safe person to express them to.

Designed to Be Real

We are designed to be real, not to live in a false self. Real, for one thing, means honest. It means admitting that something is wrong, even if you don't know what it is. It means that underneath your façade, you become willing to acknowledge that you are not the person you are attempting to portray yourself as. Being real means recognizing that there are things about how you are living that are not satisfying. It means accepting that you are going to need help. This is important because you cannot heal and grow by yourself. We are made to learn and grow and develop through relationships. It takes tremendous courage to be real!

Good news! The abandoned real self is not dead. Your heart may be shriveled, crushed, cringing, beaten down, and defeated—but your heart is not dead. The spark of life that is you comes from your Creator, and the real you is as resilient as the flowers that bloom again each springtime! (See "Coming Out of Hiding" in the Appendix.) You are going to need help to recover. "Help" is a really big no-no for the false self. The false self believes that the best way to handle life is to be strong, independent, able to take care of yourself, and stay in control—no matter what. We very often travel down a lot of dead end routes before the false self is ready to soften a bit and consider that there may be other ways to win the war against pain.

What the abandoned self needs is love, and that means relationship. This takes different forms for different people. Some people find their way to a love relationship with God, but stay away from people. Others are able to find a safe person or group to begin to be real with. One relationship that is absolutely vital is the relationship with yourself. There is a saying that, "it's never too late to have a happy childhood." As we begin to receive the nurturing we have always needed, we can start to love and appreciate our own self.

The Scripture says to "love your neighbor as you love yourself" (Mark 12:31). Loving yourself can become an intentional journey. You can refuse to hate yourself, even if you don't yet understand all that is going on within you. You can give yourself a pat on the back, tell yourself you have done a good job, forgive yourself if you mess up, remind yourself that mistakes are good—that's the way we learn. You can make it your business to find safe people whom you can learn to trust with your real heart issues.

Mistakes are good—that's the way we learn.

It is important to develop the skill of asking yourself questions and learning to listen to your own heart. Here are some examples:

- How am I feeling right now?

- What do I want?

- What do I like? What makes me feel good?

- What don't I like? What makes me feel uncomfortable?

This is not selfish. It is essential. It is learning to be real, and you have the courage to do that. It's part of the package of who you really are.

When we don't receive the nurturing we need, we can become stuck developmentally. It is important to remember that on any level where we are stuck, we can pick up right there and begin again to grow and heal and thrive.

CHAPTER FIVE

Sensitivity

For a sensitive child, the wounds of abuse and rejection (especially rejection) can be more painful than for children who have other types of gifts. A sensitive child has the gift of being a connector, one who loves people and loves bringing them together. A sensitive child is designed to bring a sense of belonging and joy to their family and friends. It is exquisitely painful for a sensitive child to be abandoned, ridiculed, or belittled. And because the sensitive child is more aware of people's feelings and needs, they are more likely to wander into areas of relationship that push people's buttons. The often confusing result is being on the receiving end of people's defensive reactions.

A sensitive child's natural inclination will be to help, to bring relief when someone is hurting. Oftentimes the parents will not be attuned to their own feelings or needs, and will feel threatened by their child's awareness of their vulnerability. This may lead to intense rejection of the child. Also, if a parent is not aware of their own woundedness and need for attention and healing, they may react with disapproval and disconnect when the child expresses similar needs and feelings.

A sensitive child often grows up with only a vague sense of why they feel so left out and so different. The sensitive child can become the scapegoat, taking the brunt of the family's rejection for their real feelings of vulnerability, and need for acceptance and love. If no caring adult has helped the child to understand and put words to all of this, the child will have no realization of why they feel such a helpless sense of rejection.

A sensitive child is susceptible to codependency (which we will discuss in depth in a later chapter). If their own feelings and needs are not genuinely appreciated, attended to and nurtured, the child will experience an abandoned self, made even more intense because of their sensitive nature. The response to this painful state of affairs is often to become a little "helper," trying to find a sense of acceptance by helping or fixing other people. This is codependency and is a malfunction of the gift of sensitivity. It positions the child toward a lifelong addiction to becoming enmeshed in other people's problems, to the exclusion of having his or her own needs acknowledged and met.

It is vital for the sensitive person to realize that their sensitivity is a gift and a treasure, to intentionally reject codependency, and to seek out people who will appreciate, nurture, and mentor them in the healing and true blossoming of this beautiful gift.

Sensitivity is a gift and a treasure.

CHAPTER SIX

Defenses

Denial ain't just a river in Egypt.

MARK TWAIN

We all have areas in which we live in denial. Denial is a psychological defense that keeps us from being aware of a painful area in our life. Denial is a blind spot. Denial can be partial or complete. The more overwhelming the original trauma, the more complete the denial.

Many years ago I read an article in a Canadian newspaper about a couple who had a disabled little girl. They had four caretakers for the child. At some point they realized that the child was being abused by one of the caretakers. They set up a video camera, and indeed found that one of the women who had been caring for their child was abusing her. The woman was arrested and placed in custody. Even after she herself had seen the videos, she insisted that she had not abused the child. Denial can run very deep.

Denial can take the form of many different kinds of defenses. Defenses are long ingrained habit patterns whose purpose is to keep us from experiencing or being aware of overwhelming painful emotions. Defenses are the behavior patterns of the false self. These patterns are often unconscious, formed at an early age, initially involuntary, and can be quite resistant to change. We all have them. It is important to identify defenses for what they are—ways to avoid feeling devastated. We ought not to call these defenses good or normal when they are keeping us stuck in trauma-based behaviors. What kept you safe as a child, may be keeping you stuck as an adult!

> *Defenses are the behavior patterns of the false self.*

Overeating is a major defense. Children so often find their only comfort in food when things are distressing all around them. Masturbation is another way for a child to feel good when in distress. Food and masturbation are some of the only ways a child can feel some relief, and these can become lifelong addictions.

Another defense is talking too much. This is called a verbal defense. If you keep talking it can prevent you from feeling your emotions. Staying busy (workaholism) is another way to prevent yourself from being in touch with your feelings. People who stay busy all the time are often trying to "be good" and to find a sense of acceptance and worth by "doing the right thing." If this is a defense, it means that it is coming from a place of avoiding real feelings.

Another common defense is "clinging." A person who has an "abandoned self" may cling to other people in order to find a sense of identity. This will always be a false identity. You cannot find resolution for a lack of self by clinging to another person. Some people like being clung to. They are codependent and find a false sense of identity by feeling needed. Both clinging and codependency are defenses. Both come from a lack of nurture and a deep internal sense of feeling empty, alone, and abandoned. Marital stress often comes from two people trying to cling to each other for a sense of identity and acceptance. As one friend said, "two ticks, no dog."

If you want to heal and grow, a good exercise is to practice sitting still and being quiet. Sometimes this can be quite challenging, like facing a giant. It is amazing how hard it can be to just sit. You can begin by doing this for just a minute or two if it feels overwhelming. This is a way to practice being real, to practice facing whatever in you feels overwhelming. Take the challenge! Gradually increase the time until you can spend time with yourself. Notice what comes up when you are quiet.

A further exercise is to doodle. Simply let yourself do anything you want on paper. If you notice what you're thinking or feeling, doodle it. Let different parts of your self express different points of view. Add a word or two as you go. Have fun with it!

Another thing that can help is to talk about what you are going through. Find a safe person to talk to. Your spirit has the resilience and strength to face this battle of becoming real.

Defenses are a pattern of behavior adopted to help you survive overwhelming emotions. They come from a "false self" and are designed to avoid our "true self." One of my friends said "when the "good" part of us (the false self) can begin to acknowledge and embrace what feels "bad" in us (which are overwhelming feelings), that's when healing begins to take place."

Can you think of some other defenses? All addictions, isolating, rage-aholic behavior, obsessing, staying numb, hoarding, self-hatred, controlling behaviors, living in fantasy, criticizing self or others, laughing when talking about painful feelings, blaming others, ridicule, showing off, trying to be perfect ... I tell you, the list goes on and on. But we are not meant to live in a defensive false self. We are meant to embrace whatever pain is necessary to be our true, real, beautiful, creative and productive self ... the one that we were created to be!

We are not meant to live in a defensive false self. We are meant to embrace whatever pain is necessary to be our true, real, beautiful, creative and productive self.

When you let go of your defenses, you are left with the reality of your innermost feelings. This takes time and is usually a gradual process. It is so important to be honest about these tender emotions. These are the feelings which you have been left alone with. These are the trauma emotions. These are the places in which you feel "bad." These are the areas where you need help. Being honest about your feelings and your needs is such an important and healthy step. It truly takes courage to be real!

"Come to the edge," he said.
"But we're afraid," they said.
"Come to the edge," he said.
"But we'll fall!" they said.
"Come to the edge," he said.
And they came.
And he pushed them.
And they flew.

CHRISTOPHER LOGUE

CHAPTER SEVEN

Codependency

Molly was a really "nice" person. She was always bringing blankets or food to the homeless. She had lots of friends, and would go out of her way to be there for them if they needed her—to take them to the hospital, shopping, or just to be there if they needed to talk about their problems. She felt it was selfish of her to even think about saying no. Molly always seemed to be busy. She had little sense of her own identity apart from being a really good helper. She rarely talked about herself, or revealed what was going on in her own heart. She was chronically tired, and would occasionally wonder how to get off the merry-go-round.

Codependency is a very important issue when it comes to being real. Codependency will steal your time, energy, and purpose in life. Codependency is inappropriate caretaking of others. Codependency means being dependent upon another's approval instead of loving and functioning out of your true self. Codependency is being excessively concerned with the needs of others, and a decreased ability to appropriately attend to your own needs. Codependency is also known as "relationship addiction."

When someone is up, you are up. When someone is down, you are down. A co-dependent person allows themself to be manipulated by others. Codependent people usually have suppressed anger (anger that has never been safely expressed and understood). Codependency comes from a false self.

Telltale signs of codependency can be:

- difficulty saying "no" to the requests of others without feeling guilty and the accompanying weariness of soul,

- finding yourself with very little time for yourself,

- having a continual sense of being overwhelmed,

- feeling "good" when you can be helping others or fixing difficult situations, but feeling uneasy or uncomfortable with down time,

- always seeming to be on the giving end with little receiving,

- and wishing that you could find a way to stop the dizzying pace of life.

Codependency comes from Type A Trauma (the absence of adequate nurturing), and often involves deep seated feelings of abandonment. The purpose of codependent behavior is to avoid the abandonment feelings. When a child has been emotionally abandoned, whether from parental illness, absence, or dysfunction, that child's spirit so often feels forsaken, neglected, and alone. This is one of the most painful of experiences, because we are meant to be connected in love. In order to compensate for the abandonment, the child will tend to want to help the parent, to seek for approval and acceptance through meeting the needs of the caretaker. **The focus here is external, on satisfying the needs of others, rather than coming from a true heart connection.**

The beginnings of a codependent lifestyle often occur within an atmosphere of fear and uncertainty. By helping or trying to meet the needs of a parent, so that they calm down or feel better, the child tries to be accepted. Otherwise things don't feel so good, and a child cannot process those overwhelming feelings without the help of a healthy adult. Without a healing process, these patterns we learn in childhood persist throughout our adult life.

The healing process will involve awareness of the pain of having an abandoned true self. It is not fulfilling to be codependent. It is not secure to live life as a false self. It may feel safe, but there is no sense of joy, no sense of accomplishment, no sense of the true self. It is rather like a treadmill that you can't seem to get off. We are not meant to be codependent. We are created to know ourselves deeply, to appreciate the unique talents and gifts that are our birthright, and to develop these talents in creative and satisfying arenas of our lives. Codependency will steal your birthright. Codependency is a problem that we are meant to solve. It needs attention and pursuit of the truth—the truth about who you are and all that you were created to be!

We are created to know ourselves deeply, to appreciate the unique talents and gifts that are our birthright.

There are many resources to help you in this battle. Support groups are remarkably valuable. Search them out. I encourage you to read about codependency, a little each day. It will reframe your thinking. A daily devotional on codependent themes will help to reacquaint you with healthy relational principles. And pray! Pray for the Lord to open your eyes and to show you truth about any codependent relationships that you are involved in. Ask Him to show you the codependent patterns. And ask Him to show you the path of life. Ask and keep asking!

Lord, show me the codependent patterns in my life. Show me the truth about codependency and the truth of who You created me to be. Help me to be honest and open with myself, with others, and with You. Lead me into the healthy relationships and into the creative and rewarding life that You have designed for me.

CHAPTER EIGHT

Anger

There are two aspects to anger. Anger is an emotion, but anger can also be a defense. It is important to distinguish which type of anger you are dealing with. Some of the feelings we've been talking about are painful, crushing, overwhelming feelings. Feelings like being trapped or helpless, terrified or abandoned. Feelings in which you feel small and alone. With anger you tend to feel strong and in control. So, often our brains choose to feel angry instead of feeling hopeless or scared or rejected. This type of anger is a defense, a way to avoid being real in our pain. This is especially true if unhealthy expressions of anger were modeled for you as a child by someone who was supposed to be taking care of you. We learn by example. And we often take on the defensive actions of those who are near and dear to us.

Defensive Anger

Violent behavior is not an expression of angry emotions. It is a defense. Yelling, screaming, throwing and breaking things are signs that a person is actually not in touch with their painful emotions. Defensive anger can be expressed in numerous other, less obvious ways such as isolating, pouting, silence, blaming, being late or failing to keep commitments. All of these behaviors are ways of passively expressing defensive anger and are used to defend against the vulnerable emotions of feeling overwhelmed, hopeless, powerless, and so on.

This defensive anger is a protection for a hurting child. It is normal for human beings to hide in this way. But what kept us safe as a child often keeps us stuck as an adult. The thing about defensive anger is that it keeps you from being real and vulnerable, and ultimately keeps you from the healing you need in order to grow and become all you were created to be. Defensive anger distances you from yourself, from others, and from God. It will keep you in a place of emotional isolation.

Defensive anger distances you from yourself, from others, and from God.

Ultimately, it is important to let go of the defensive anger. This is usually a gradual process as you learn to experience your vulnerable emotions (feeling helpless, scared, trapped, hopeless, ashamed) within the framework of a safe relationship and/or a safe group of people. It is important to have mature people to help you sort out what you are feeling. This involves a willingness to be real, to express real emotions. It usually calls for the learning of a new language—the language of emotions. And it takes faith. Because you have not seen things work out well in emotionally difficult situations, there is no experience of being vulnerable and being okay. It's like going to a new country. You find out about it from others who have been there, but then you have the option of going there yourself. It is always a challenge to give up anger. I have found it helpful to say, "I give up this anger. I am willing to be vulnerable." There is a learning process of becoming tender and gentle with others, but especially with yourself.

Suppressed Anger

The other type of anger problem has to do with suppression. When you put the letter "d" on the word anger, it spells danger. If expressing the emotion of anger was a dangerous or unsafe experience for you as a child, you may have suppressed anger or rage and locked it inside. If this is the case, you are likely to be overly "nice" and helpful to others, or to be always trying to be "good." You may have anger always coming out sideways as sarcastic remarks or critical joking. Or, you may have somatic symptoms, meaning that your anger is being held unconsciously in a certain part of your body causing physical symptoms, for example, headaches, stomach aches, or muscle tension.

Suppressed anger needs to come out front-ways within a trusting relationship with someone who is safe. It is important to be able to express the anger in words, to talk about who it was originally directed toward, and to come to an understanding of why you feel/felt that way. It is vital to experience anger and realize that you are not a bad person because you are angry. The part of you that has been locked inside in anger or rage needs to be brought to the surface, expressed and integrated into the rest of your personality. This can be quite a scary process. I have found that it helps to talk with someone who is good at handling suppressed emotions. As one friend says,

"When the 'good' part of you can begin to accept the 'bad' part of you, healing begins to occur." Ultimately, it can be a great relief to go through this process, and it can free you up in all sorts of ways: to have more energy, more joy in life, better relationships, better health, and being able to feel comfortable with yourself.

Whether the issue is defensive anger or suppressed anger, there is a path through the wilderness. Or, maybe it is up to you to create a new path. I believe that there are solutions to every challenge, and that we are created to find the solutions!

CHAPTER NINE

Identification With the Abuser

The way that we are treated as children is the way that we learn to treat ourselves. If a parent is critical and harsh or angry, the child will "download" the same qualities into a part of themselves. Basically children behave toward themselves in the same manner in which the parent dealt with them. This can be quite subtle. A child may vow, "I'll never be anything like my mother," and spend a lot of time and energy developing the opposite qualities. However, when push comes to shove (when the stress level is high), we generally default to our deepest layers of learned behavior.

Any destructive patterns we have learned from our caretakers during times of high distress become hard-wired into us. We will find ourselves reacting in similar ways when we are stressed. We can have a highly self-critical or angry part, and this is often unconscious.

When something is unconscious it will continue to function until it is brought into awareness. Only then can it be addressed and modified.

I worked with a woman who had not spoken to her mother for years, because of her mother's excessively religious, punitive, belittling, abusive way of relating. We worked together toward her being able to have compassion and love for herself. I remember one session in which we were getting close to the feelings of helplessness and abandonment, when she began to say things about herself such as, "I ought to know better than to think I'm worth anything ... I must be having problems because I haven't obeyed God ... It's my own fault that I'm having trouble ... If I weren't so stupid and defective, I wouldn't be in this mess ..." These were things that her mother had spoken to her time and again when she was a child, and she had incorporated these words into her beliefs about herself.

Agreement with the abuser is a safety measure, a defense.

Agreement with the abuser is a safety measure, a defense. If you beat yourself down, then maybe the beating you get from the abuser won't be as bad. If you agree with the abuser's reality, maybe that person will finally come to accept and like you. How can you stand up for yourself when there is no one to help you see that the abuser's reality is not the only reality there is?

The healing process involves taking the risk to feel, and then to identify the emotions that you felt during the times of abuse—whether that abuse was sexual, physical or verbal. I personally believe that verbal abuse can be worse than physical abuse because the words that are spoken can become deep wounds that last long after physical wounds have mended. Part of the process involves breaking all agreements with the abuser (such as refusing to call yourself stupid), and coming to understand why you have felt and acted in certain patterned ways. It always involves coming to the place where you can tolerate, understand, and have compassion for yourself when you feel hopeless, rejected, and afraid. Learning to love yourself is so, so, so important … and provides you with the courage to be real!

CHAPTER TEN

Being Religious

O ne of the ways people who believe in God get stuck is by being religious. By religious, I mean doing what you think you should be doing, or what you think God expects of you, and following all the rules, but not actually being in relationship with God. Being religious is being led by your head, instead of being led by your heart/spirit! This is yet another example of a false identity—not being your real self.

We were created to have a relationship with God, to be a part of God's big family! But so often we project our feelings and beliefs about our parents, particularly our father, onto God. We try to do what we think He wants of us, and we hide away in shame the feelings and needs that have not been acceptable to our parents. We feel that we cannot approach God unless and until we correct all our "bad" behaviors and meet the standards that our parents have insisted upon.

God wants us to be real and honest with Him. God is a Person and we are people, created to be like Him. When you are someone's child, you are like them. We are God's children, designed to take after our Abba (an intimate term for God as Father). What does that look like? How are we to be like Him? I think it means that we are designed to be loving, creative, brilliantly intelligent, forgiving, compassionate, funny, kind, honest, full of joy, patient and enduring, brave, adventuresome, fearless, innocent and good. Well, that's just a short list. Basically, it's everything our hearts desire. We are children of God!

Being religious is human. It's trying to be made acceptable by our performance. If you are running around doing all the right things, trying to be perfect, but feeling burnt out, exhausted and depleted, you may be stuck in religion—rules without relationship. If this is the case, you will never feel "good enough" to be loved and accepted by God. Please understand that His love and acceptance of you come without any strings attached, it is unconditional. He loves you because His nature is love—He can't *not* love you!

God wants us to share the deep feelings of our heart with Him. A friend of mine was sick for quite a long time, and not getting better despite trying to trust God, pray, and do all the right things. At one point she got really angry at God and accused Him of not helping her. Shortly afterward she began to recover. There is something about empty rituals that blocks our ability to receive. Being honest and open allows us to fully experience and receive the goodness of God and all He has for us. That is hard for us human beings. It would feel easier to us if we had a formula to follow, a "to do" list to tackle. True relationship with God takes time to build and time to experience.

God's love is not about "doing" anything. It's about "being" His child and receiving His love. God wants us to receive His acceptance and love as a gift. That means you can't earn it. You just receive His love and ask for more.

> *God's love is not about "doing" anything. It's about "being" His child and receiving His love.*

Try being honest with God. Tell Him how you feel, how you see things. Talk about the questions you have, the things that don't make any sense to you. Ask God to show you what is real and true, what He had in mind when He created you. Ask your Abba what it means to be His child!

CHAPTER ELEVEN

Mania and Depression

I want to say a few words about the concepts of mania and depression. In no way do I mean to imply that Bipolar Disorder is not a physical, brain disorder. It is. Medication is important in helping people to cope with this devastating illness. However, I have found that there is also a psychological dynamic inherent in the cycles of mania and depression, and that addressing this component can lead to a marked decrease in these cycles.

In short, mania is a defense. I have found it to be an involuntary, automatic way that the brain shields itself from the overwhelming feelings of psychological abandonment. This psychological abandonment—that aching aloneness—is what we call depression. When a child does not have the parental help he or she needs to deal with overwhelming feelings, that child experiences a desperate sense of isolation and despair, which we call abandonment. It is an overwhelmingly awful feeling, impossible for a child to navigate without words and without support.

My understanding of mania is that when something good happens, or a child experiences happiness (whether that happiness is from a real or fantasized source), the brain latches on to the good feelings and magnifies them into a hyped-up sense of feeling really, really great. The brain hangs onto those feelings as long as possible because the alternative, the abandonment depression, is literally too much to bear. At some point, however, something will trigger the brain to feel those abandonment feelings, and then the person is catapulted out of their "happy high" and back into the depression phase.

The brain latches on to the good feelings and magnifies them into a hyped-up sense of feeling really, really great.

Both of these phases can be addressed psychologically, in therapy. For the depression phase, the person can learn to move toward the feelings of abandonment, instead of staying as far as possible away from them. A person can learn to open up to the devastating feelings inside, to understand why they feel that way (because they have been abandoned psychologically) and to begin to find the nurture and sustenance that they need. In essence, depression deepens when we try to escape the abandonment feelings inside. To the "inner child" this just compounds the feelings of abandonment, and the person sinks deeper into despair.

For the manic phase, the person can learn that mania is a defense, a habitual way that their brain has learned to try to manage the abandonment/depression feelings. Mania destabilizes the brain, however, and can lead to an out of control spiral into an arena of unreality. Although manic tendencies are initially involuntary, a person can learn to pull themselves back from becoming manic, and choose instead to face and deal with the abandonment feelings. I would say that having someone to help you with this is vital. It is just too hard to manage alone. As a person learns to pull back from the manic feelings and connect with, understand, and work through the abandonment depression, the cycles of mania and depression will even out and can potentially resolve.

In the chapter on Stories, I tell about Sally, who came to see me because of a long history of the severe moods swings of Bipolar Disorder. Sally described her abandonment (which she would experience in her depressive phases) like this: "I keep thinking that I'm a bad person. I feel indifferent to people. I don't feel that attachment to my family. When my mother didn't attach to me I thought it was my fault. I could never show my emotions in front of my mom … she wouldn't let me. I feel 'bad' if I have negative thoughts. When I don't feel depressed I feel elated. I feel 'good' when I can please people. I feel so down in the dumps if I'm not helpful. I feel like I hinder people. I always want to make people happy—that's the only way I can accept myself."

So Sally would have depression phases where she would feel worthless and bad, and manic phases where she would be exceptionally helpful and hence, acceptable and good. As she has learned to identify both her manic and depressive tendencies and the motivating forces behind each one, her cycles have decreased markedly. She is learning to be real, to receive the help she needs, and to love and nurture herself.

Answers

"... ask for the old paths, where the good way is, and walk in it; then you will find rest for your souls ..."

JEREMIAH 6:16, NKJV

CHAPTER TWELVE

Feel to Heal

The Importance of Your Emotions

One of the things I frequently find myself saying is "feel to heal." It is important to be connected to your feelings in order for the healing to happen. When you are feeling, your heart is open. Your feelings come from what you believe, and your beliefs come from what you have experienced. It looks like this:

Experience > Belief > Feeling

In order for your feelings to change, your beliefs need to change. And in order for your beliefs to change, it's important to be in a place to experience your feelings, not just to be thinking about them, but to experience those feelings in a new way. According to Dr. Jim Wilder, our most basic beliefs about ourselves and others are generally in place by the age of eighteen months. Whenever we have experiences that involve overwhelming emotions, we need someone to help us to put words to our feelings, to feel safe with those feelings, and to come to understand what has happened to us. When we have someone to help us process these events, the brain files that experience and we can draw upon it in the future for help with similar experiences.

Earlier we discussed that if we don't have someone to help us with what feels overwhelming, the experience does not get processed, and does not get filed. Instead, it gets suppressed or locked inside, walled off with the overwhelming feelings still pulsating. The brain then goes into "defense mode," where it gets engaged in thinking as a way to avoid feeling. Many, many of us live in our heads as a way to avoid our hearts. But it is in our hearts that our "real self" lives, the part of us that feels, that loves, that hates, that engages in real life as opposed to fantasy life.

Negative experiences become negative beliefs: "I'm not good enough, I'm not loveable, I'm stupid, etc." In order to heal those beliefs it is necessary to feel the emotions, at least to some degree. Not only is it important to feel them, but to feel them in the company of a safe and caring person. It is important to put words to those feelings and to come to an understanding of what we feel and why we feel that way. This is a process. It takes time and growth and understanding, little by little.

Negative experiences become negative beliefs.

This process is an awakening. It is awakening to who you are, what you feel, and what you need. It's about the you-ness of you! Ideally your mom is the one who initially sees, experiences, encourages, and celebrates who "you" are. Hopefully dad is there to welcome you into your identity as separate from mom. But we live in a fallen world. So often our moms are not as emotionally or physically available as we need them to be, and our dads are themselves hurting and broken. But our Creator says, *"When my father and my mother abandon me, the Lord will take care of me"* (Psalm 27:10, NLT). I believe that our Creator is in the active process of re-parenting each and every one of us. We are learning how to cooperate with that process. You were created to have deep, intimate, lasting relationships with others where you can "be yourself" and be cherished for who you are. You are designed to live and love from a pure and innocent heart.

You may have had times when you felt that you were not quite yourself. It is so important to notice those times and to ask yourself, "What was I feeling?" and "What happened to bring this on?" "Did I feel safe to express myself? Did I feel that I needed to impress someone? What might have happened had I been more real'?"

It is also helpful to be in the company of people who are actively engaged in a healing lifestyle. That is why groups like the "A" groups (AA, NA, OA) are so valuable. You get to hear and see people being real, putting words onto painful experiences, and to hear what they have learned about resolving difficult issues in healthy ways. This is a good way to develop an emotional vocabulary: being able to put appropriate words to a wide range of feelings.

Talking to a friend or counselor is another good way to become more aware of your feelings and needs. There is evidence that speaking about your experiences helps your brain to become conscious of your feelings in a way that is very different from just thinking about them.

Writing is also very valuable to the process. The words themselves actually help our brain to reflect, to understand, and to become competent at self-awareness. It is vitally important to be self-aware.

Otherwise we may be like those in this quote from Thoreau: "The mass of men lead lives of quiet desperation."

We are all in the process of becoming who we were created to be. It takes work, it takes risk, it takes practice, and it takes people who will love you and listen to you and give you honest feedback. Don't settle for "quiet desperation." Desire the best. Desire to be all you can be. Open your heart to dream again. Feel to heal!

CHAPTER THIRTEEN

Jesus Our Healer

"Come to me, all you who are weary and burdened, and I will give you rest. Take my yoke upon you and learn from me, for I am gentle and humble in heart, and you will find rest for your souls."

JESUS IN MATTHEW 11:28-29 (NIV)

This may be a familiar Scripture to many of us. In my experience it is literally true. When we come to Jesus with our hurts and anguish, He is there to heal us. He wants us to come. His desire is to heal us and to show us how very much He loves us. The challenge for us in this is twofold. The first is being honest with ourselves. Most of us are so used to living in denial and functioning with defenses that we don't acknowledge our pain to ourselves. We may not even be aware of our need for healing. When our difficult emotions are triggered, we do our best to stuff them back in so that we don't feel them. We feel ashamed that we can't handle things on our own.

The second challenge is believing that Jesus is who He says He is and believing that He loves us. The Bible calls Jesus the "Everlasting Father." For those of us who have had a painful relationship with our own fathers, or have had no father, it can seem unimaginable that there would be a God who could be a loving Father to us. We project our beliefs about our own fathers onto God.

For both of these reasons, it is helpful to have someone assist you with bringing your wounded heart to Jesus. A sensitive mentor can encourage you to tune in to the difficult emotions. They can give you the message that what you are feeling is real and important, and that you are not bad. It is also incredibly valuable to have someone who knows Jesus as a loving Father. They can pray for Jesus to help you when you feel like you are overwhelmed and drowning. It's kind of like landing an airplane in a wild storm. You have to know where you are headed and to maintain the course for your destination despite the turbulent buffeting of the winds.

I remember the first time that I experienced Jesus coming to the aid of someone in trouble. I was working with a young man, Andy, who was experiencing a lot of anxiety. As I helped him to turn within and to focus in on his feelings, he began to describe how distressed he had felt as a young boy when his parents would fight and scream at each other. He desperately wanted to find a way to help them, yet he was powerless to do anything about it. His belief was that when people (even in his present life) were angry, he was unsafe and helpless. I asked him to listen for the truth. He immediately started crying. I asked him what he was seeing and he said that Jesus was standing in front of him with His arms outstretched. He ran into those loving arms and told me that he felt safe for the first time in his life!

Scripture tells us that God is omnipresent. That means He is present in all times and places. When we awaken to His presence with us, even in a memory, we can be aware of His love and His healing thoughts. Psalm 139 (KJV) says, "How precious also are thy thoughts unto me, O God! how great is the sum of them! If I should count them, they are more in number than the sand …" I believe that this awakening to "God with us" (one of the names of God, which is Emmanuel) is what this journey of life is all about, and that we are all learning to recognize and come into a deep and loving relationship with God. As one song says, "I will open up my heart and let the Healer set me free."

When people bring their overwhelming pain to God, they come to find that God is with them and cares immensely about what is happening to them. Our beliefs come from our experiences. When we are able to perceive God with us in painful places or memories, His love and caring and what He communicates to us there can completely change our beliefs and hence, the feelings. Sometimes it is a long, long journey to get there. We all have our defenses. How do we trust again? So often it feels impossible. But, our Creator has foreseen our pain and struggles. He knows how hard it is for us to trust again.

As Simon Tugwell reminds us:

So long as we imagine that it is we who have to look for God, we must often lose heart. But it is the other way about. He is looking for us. And so we can recognize that very often we are not looking for God; far from it, we are in full flight from Him, in high rebellion against Him. And He knows that and has taken it into account. He has followed us into our own darkness; there, where we thought finally to escape Him, we run straight into His arms. So we do not have to erect a false piety for ourselves, to give us the hope of salvation. Our hope is in His determination to save us, and He will not give in.[1]

Endnote:

1.   *The Sacred Romance* (p. 81). Simon Tugwell.

CHAPTER FOURTEEN

The Stories

The following are true life stories of people with whom I have
worked. My usual practice is to see someone on a weekly basis.
It generally takes some time to form a trusting relationship. It may
take time for a person to be able to tune into their emotions, which
allows them to be present—to be real. If there has been spiritual
abuse (abuse by religious leaders), or if a person has warped images of
God, it will take time to work these through as well. It takes time to
form a trusting relationship with God.

I generally work with a person for several months, often longer.
People who make the greatest progress are, in most cases, those
who have a good support system. I encourage people to engage in
a recovery groups, such as AA, NA, OA, Celebrate Recovery, and
particularly groups focused on codependency. I also encourage
people to read on codependency as an adjunct to therapy, as I

have found codependency to be a major block to being real. The most important thing in finding a counselor to work with is this: do you feel safe and comfortable with the person? What is your "gut reaction" to them? Remember, recovery is a process and it is important to stay with the process.

To encourage you in your own journey, I wanted to share some stories of others who have already walked down that path of exploring and becoming their real self. I have changed their names to protect their identity, but each story is true and involves real people. Here they are.

Overcoming Fear

I worked with a woman who believed she had a sexually transmitted disease (STD). She didn't have one—we had had her tested numerous times—but the testing did not help to ease her fears. One day I asked her if she would be willing to ask Jesus to help her with this. She agreed, so we prayed for the Lord to bring healing. As I was praying for her, she had an impression of herself as a newborn baby. She had been adopted, and in the scene she saw herself being placed in a basinet. She had the sense that that baby felt extremely abandoned and rejected. I asked her to look for Jesus there. She did so and then reported that He was with her and holding her.

She relished feeling safe and secure, and felt that God was telling her that He had always wanted her and that she belonged to Him. When we ended the session, I asked her about the STD. For the first time she told me that she definitely did not have an STD. It was something of a shock to me to hear her say that, as no amount of my trying to convince her before had ever helped! The belief that she had an STD never returned after that session.

Resolving Anxiety

Debbie had trouble sitting at the dinner table with her family. She liked to eat alone, but would become anxious if she had to eat with others. As we explored her anxiety, she remembered that as a child her father would force her to eat, at times pushing the food into her mouth. She felt overwhelmed, trapped, and extremely fearful as she unpacked this memory. I encouraged her to look for Jesus in that scenario. As she did, she came to the place where she felt Him holding her and comforting her, even as her father was thrusting the food at her. This was a healing for her. Subsequently, she reported feeling quite comfortable in being able to eat in the company of other people.

She felt Him holding her and comforting her ...

Somehow, when we can sense the Lord's presence with us, even though the circumstances don't change, our perception of ourself does change. Our belief about what happened changes and our beliefs about ourself change. When we know that we are not alone and that we are loved, the experience is no longer a trauma. The beliefs and feelings resolve with that understanding. It can be a scary journey getting there, but once we can sense the Lord's presence with us, the trauma-based beliefs are erased for good!

Uncovering a Trigger

Millie had been coming to see me for several weeks. After some initial discussion, she seemed unaware of the need for any further exploration and was content to just chat with me. I asked her if there was anything else she wanted to work on. After long thought, she mentioned that she had joined a gym to exercise, but had not been able to get herself to go. She thought this was odd because she liked to exercise. I asked her if she would be willing to ask her "self" why she didn't want to go. I suggested that perhaps there was a part of her that was rejecting the idea. If you have one foot on the gas, and one foot on the brake, the brake wins. If part of her wanted to go (gas pedal), and part of her refused (brake pedal), she would never make it to they gym!

She listened inside for a few minutes and heard, "It's too much of an effort." She immediately dismissed that idea (which is like telling the child inside to shut up), saying that it's not a big effort because she enjoys exercise. I asked her to just hang in there and listen without telling herself that what she was hearing was stupid. She then heard, "It's hard meeting new people." Again, she felt this was not true of her—she generally liked meeting new people. I asked her if she would be willing to ask this "part" of her who she is: "What part of me is saying this?"

She was willing and asked herself the question. After a few quiet moments she said, "Now I'm going back to being a kid. I'm in the school band and I'm going to a concert … I'm nervous about being in front of so many kids. I upchucked all over my red dress and my mother said she was not going to dress me again … I'm crying."

I asked her if she would be willing to look for Jesus in that scenario. (Since Jesus is "omnipresent"—in all times and places, He is and was there with her.) She told me she was willing and when I asked her what Jesus was doing she said, "He's holding me." Millie experienced feeling comforted in this memory, an experience in which she had originally felt frightened and overwhelmed about being in front of a lot of people. This belief (that she couldn't perform) was being triggered by the prospect of going to the gym in her present life. When she felt the love of Jesus and knew that she was not alone, this healed the memory, changed the belief. The next week she tried going to the gym again. Afterward she came in with a big smile saying, "I did it!" Trauma occurred when she went through an overwhelming experience alone. When she experienced the comfort and love of Jesus in the trauma memory, it was no longer a trauma.

Releasing Trauma

Jeanne was going to take a bus trip to see her daughter who lived two and a half hours away. She said she could not drive that distance by herself because of severe anxiety. This she related to a car accident she had experienced 17 years prior, and she had not been able to drive long distances by herself since that time. The accident had caused a significant head trauma with headaches and scar tissue. She had not been able to lift her left arm for 6 months following the collision. Jeanne felt angry at the man who had caused the accident. She was bitter and had a lot of fear. As we talked about this, she was crying and trembling. We gently invited the Lord into the scene of the accident. Jeanne was able to say a prayer forgiving the man who had hit her car. I asked the Lord to take away the anger, bitterness and fear, and to bless Jeanne with what He wanted to give her. She quickly sensed His presence with her and within a few minutes she was smiling broadly. She rested in His presence and afterward said that she felt wonderful. She later reported that she had no fear about driving to her daughter's house.

Addressing Abandonment

My friend Michael recently came to visit me. He has struggled with depression and alcohol abuse for years. He told me that he and his wife essentially had no physical relationship. Their interactions were superficial and distant. Michael felt bitter and resentful that his wife was not meeting his needs. He felt that he had to almost beg her to be with him, and that she resisted his efforts. I talked to Michael about the importance of not looking to someone outside of yourself to meet your needs. "It is so important to take responsibility for your own pain and your own needs," I said. I knew that many members of his family had been emotionally abandoned as children.

I talked to Michael about the "little boy" who had experienced abandonment. "That little boy is (metaphorically) inside of you, still feeling alone and unnurtured. He lives in a cold, dark, lonely world inside. When we cling to other people to fill our needs, that is a way to avoid the little boy's feelings. The only one who can really give him what he needs now is you! He needs you to turn toward him (inside) and say 'I hear you, I understand that you are feeling alone, I'm here with you, I'm learning to listen to you.'"

I suggested that Michael place his hands over his heart as he spoke to the "little one." I said, "Acknowledging the 'real you' which feels hurt and alone positions you for healing. When you turn toward your own pain, it opens the door for Jesus to bring His help. Our choices, and how we talk to ourselves, either opens the door for healing or closes it tight. When you turn toward other people or things to ease your pain, it doesn't work and you end up frustrated, addicted and codependent. Like the song says, 'lookin' for love in all the wrong places.' You cannot solve an internal problem with an external solution."

Turning to other people or things to ease your pain does not work.

I suggested to Michael that he stop looking to his wife to fill his needs and to come alongside his own heart (which is another way of saying the "little boy"). I encouraged him to practice being open to listening to his feelings and to asking Jesus for help. The prayer for help might sound like this: "Lord Jesus, I am feeling so alone and unloved. I have felt this way for such a long time. You have promised to never leave me or forsake me. Your Word says *'Even if my father and mother abandon me, the Lord will hold me close'* (Psalm 27:10, NLT). Lord, please be with me and bring what I need right now." The shorter version of this prayer is "Jesus, help!"

To my great delight, Michael called me two weeks later and said that something happened, he wasn't sure what, but that he hadn't felt depressed for a week or so, and that he was no longer demanding that his wife spend time with him. He also felt that the tension between them had lessened and he felt more of a real connection between them. Their sexual relationship still needed to be addressed, but this was a healing of Michael's abandonment pain.

I told Michael, "Depression is a word we often use as a camouflage for a deep internal sense of abandonment. As children, we are unable to tolerate those feelings, so they get locked inside and we grow up trying to do our best to exist without some of the deep basic needs of relationship. Our brains have learned to stay away from those painful feelings, because to a child, it feels like death to be so alone. We cling to others or substances to try to 'feel good,' but those feelings of abandonment are there, locked inside, capable of being triggered. When we turn toward those feelings, which is hard to do without help and guidance, we learn to tolerate, handle, and find healing for our emotions and beliefs."

In Matthew 11:28-29 (NASB) our Creator says, *"Come to Me, all you who are weary and heavy-ladened ... for I am gentle and humble in heart ... and you will find rest for your souls."*

Michael has been attending AA several times a week for the past several years. This has been tremendously supportive for him and has given him the "capacity" he has needed in order to be able to tolerate and address the painful issues in his life. Capacity is the ability to tolerate painful feelings, and it comes from having supportive and nurturing relationships. Had Michael not been attending AA, I doubt if he would have been able to make use of my suggestions to turn toward his pain and to begin the process of self-nurturing.

Facing Rejection

Lilly was a participant in one of my seminars. She defined her obstacle as "fear of failure." As I talked about emotional healing, she had a spontaneous memory of being a little girl, seeing her mother (who appeared to be overwhelmed and on edge) and asking her mom if she could help. Her mother snarled in reply, "That's all you ever want to do is help ... just get out of my hair." Lilly remembered feeling crushed by her mother's words. I encouraged her to feel the sting of it, and she started to cry, something she rarely does in public. At this point I realized that she was connecting to that rejected little girl in her heart. I asked her if she was willing to look to Jesus in that scene. She agreed to try and was able to sense Him with her, telling her that she was precious to Him and that He loved her very much. When Lilly returned to the group, she reported that her fear of being a failure simply was not there any more.

I have observed this time and again. When a person connects with a part of themselves that feels intense emotional pain and looks to Jesus for help, they find that He is present and this brings hope and healing. The beliefs that were formed in traumatic experiences are changed and healed. Sometimes it's with words, sometimes it's simply the reassurance of His presence. Often there is a memory of a childhood trauma, but not always. As a counselor, I function as a "midwife," encouraging the person to stay focused, to feel, and to ask Jesus for help in the moment. I know that healing has taken place when the person reports that what they felt and believed just a few minutes ago no longer seems true to them now. It always amazes me!

Finding Courage to Connect

Sally is a 69-year-old who came to see me because of severe mood swings, what would generally be termed Bipolar Disorder. She had been feeling suicidal for the past few months. Sally had a mother who was emotionally distant, highly critical, and verbally abusive. As a young teenager, Sally had an experience when a boy she liked, "looked at me and thought I was a freak." Since that time she had dealt daily with feelings of deep anguish about her appearance. She said, "It's constantly on my mind that I don't look normal—my face constantly changes, like it's disfigured. I always feel like I'm a freak, like people can't even look at me. I feel so rejected."

She came to the place where she was able to experience and share how utterly rejected she had felt all her life.

She always worried about people staring at her because she was so ugly (in reality she was a very pretty woman). We worked on helping her to be able to get in touch with and express her emotions. Sally courageously engaged in the process of connecting with her little abandoned self. Through deep sobs, she came to the place where she was able to experience and share how utterly rejected she had felt all her life.

Her feelings originated from very early interactions with her rejecting mother, and were replayed and solidified by the perceived rejection from the boy when she was a teen. Sally is still in the process of developing the capacity to connect with her heart and pay attention to her needs. Every time we meet, Sally is able to connect with her real emotions and experience Jesus holding her and telling her that she is beautiful and precious to Him. She is bringing more and more of her real self into the light of God's love for her. As of the present writing, she is no longer suicidal and does not experience the bipolar mood swings.

Embracing Painful Emotions

Sandy is a 60-year-old woman who has struggled for a long time with deep feelings of abandonment. The firstborn in a troubled family, she did not receive the nurturing she needed as a child in order to form a real self or be able to pay attention to her own feelings and needs. She constantly focused on the needs and feelings of others, and would feel "bad" if she asserted herself or said no to someone else. We worked on helping her connect to her "little one" (the child inside) and to be able to acknowledge and feel how utterly alone that child felt.

One time after setting a healthy boundary with another person, Sandy journaled about her feelings:

> *"I feel very bad tonight. I think it's because I turned away from trying to help _____. I feel very apart from my 'little one,' my heart. I feel very far from You, Lord. I'm so scared. I don't know how to love myself. I feel like I'm dying. Is this how a little baby feels without a mom? It feels like I'm dead inside, empty, hollow. I want to run, to get away from feeling like this. I feel like I'm a terrible person. My heart feels crushed, Lord, and it's hard to lift my eyes to You. I feel like ignoring*

this. Lord, I am not believing in You. I feel hateful and awful and so tempted to run away. Why does this keep happening to me?"

She continued writing in her journal as she felt the Lord speak to her in response: "I love you, Sandy, I am with you. Be gentle with yourself. I know where you are and I am with you and my heart is gentle toward you. Spend this time with Me and with your 'little one,' just being, just resting. Make a determination that you are going to love yourself no matter what, and not run away."

Sandy reported that when she would begin journaling she would feel emotionally shut down and separated from her own heart and from the Lord. However, when she stayed with the process she noticed that gradually she would begin to feel very close to her "little girl" (often holding a teddy bear to represent her "little one"). She would cry and feel very connected and loving toward her self. As she continued with this process, she became more and more adept at setting healthy boundaries with others, and more and more able to access and respond appropriately to her own feelings and needs.

As Sandy faced the devastating pain of her inner abandoned child and went through those moments with the Lord, she found out that she didn't die, something bad didn't happen, and the pain didn't gobble her up. This agonizing pain was the pain of a young child feeling alone in the world. When she experienced that she could get through it, she was able to build an inner strength and a strong sense of confidence within herself. She realized that she did not have to spend her life being a codependent caretaker of others for a false sense of being acceptable. She could grow, heal, and become real.

Confronting Anger

I worked with a woman, Louise, who had a very distorted view of God. She had been severely abused physically, sexually, and spiritually. Along with these terrible experiences, she had also been emotionally abandoned from the beginning. Her mother's attitude toward her was one of mocking and belittling, blaming her for all the abuse that was happening to her. Her mother also let her know that God was very unhappy with her "bad attitude" (any of her real feelings), and that she was in constant danger of eternal damnation if she didn't shape up. Louise believed that God was punishing her because she was wicked. She would say to herself, "I'm ungrateful, I'm evil, I'm bad, I'm phony, I'm hateful, I'm selfish …"

Louise was a Christian, but had a part of her that was tremendously angry at God. She told me, "It would be a mistake to ever let the angry part out." She felt that if she ever let herself be honest about how angry she was, it would confirm that she was bad and essentially, unsalvageable. It was enormously difficult for her to even consider allowing her rage toward God to be expressed. I encouraged her to draw what she was feeling, and with a great deal of encouragement, she drew herself as a big ball of hatred (toward God and everyone else). Then she drew God's face with a sadistic smile which seemed to say "Ha! … I've got you now … what you feel is sinful … I've got you nailed!"

Louise became fearful of having expressed her anger toward God, certain that it confirmed her belief that she was bad and evil. However, as we looked to the real Jesus and listened to what He had to say, she heard Him say, "I love you, Louise … I've got you." In her heart she knew this was true. Her decision to be honest with God about her rage and anger was a turning point in her recovery.

Surrending Separation Anxiety

Marie came in saying, "I have so much anxiety, I don't know where it is coming from. I think it's from being separated from my daughter. I've felt anxiety for the two years since she moved away. We were best friends. We used to do everything together. It was always her and me. We say the same things, we wear the same colors ..." She began to cry and continued, "I feel so lost without her. It's a feeling of rejection and abandonment, a feeling of being by myself."

Marie had fairly severe separation anxiety. This stemmed from a lack of secure connection with her own mother. This kind of disorder is a difficult condition to treat, generally requiring intensive counseling and, at times, medication. Marie was clinging to her daughter as a way of trying to feel whole and safe, as a way of avoiding her own feelings of abandonment.

Since Marie was very much connected with her pain, and since she had a good relationship with Jesus, we asked Him to come and bring His healing. As I prayed and she listened, Marie said, "I'm seeing that because I didn't have a mom, I formed a web around my daughter to protect her from what I didn't have. I was smothering her for what I was longing for. I was trying to give that love that I never had." Tears ran down her cheeks.

"Forgive me, Lord, for trying to smother my daughter," she prayed. As she continued to wait on the Lord, she visibly relaxed. I kept gently praying for the Lord to bring what she needed and to take away whatever was not from Him. We quietly waited for a few moments, and then she said "I'm feeling love in a whole different way. It is so calming." I smiled back at her, not uttering a word, basking in the glow of God's presence and letting His Spirit complete the work. We sat in stillness for several more minutes.

"Oh my goodness!" she exclaimed, "all of that anxiety is gone! That anxiety attachment to my daughter is all gone." She looked at me, amazement transforming her features.

I beamed back at her, excited to witness the transformation and she said, "I'm hearing, 'Marie, you just take care of yourself, I'll take care of her.'" God was speaking to her. Marie's countenance got brighter and she said, "The worrying about my daughter has let go. I was always carrying her heavy load on top of me. It is so awesome becoming myself, who I am … not dependent on everyone else. My whole breathing has even changed … the pressure is gone from my head."

At her next appointment Marie reported that she continued to have no anxiety in relation to her daughter. She confidently stated, "I am seeing things so differently since last week's session."

Awaken Your Spirit and Find Forgiveness

Jesus is with us in all times and all places. However, if our spirit is asleep or in hiding, we most likely will not be aware of His presence with us. Many of us need to have our spirit awakened and nurtured

It is important to connect to the difficult feelings because they are what the real self is experiencing.

in order to become aware of the presence of God with us. Sometimes it takes another person helping us to look for Him to or to hear what He is saying. And sometimes there are no words or pictures, but simply a sense that God is with us and that He loves us ... and then the healing comes.

If we try to forgive without connecting to our feelings, it sometimes doesn't work. It is so important to connect to the difficult feelings because they are what the real self is experiencing. When a person connects to their real self, and comes to feel loved and accepted in a place of trauma, it is usually fairly easy to forgive. Often, there are layers of trauma that need to be addressed. People sometimes wonder why they still feel angry or hurt when they have said that they forgive. If that is true for you, let me encourage you to do some further work on addressing the wounds of your heart.

To forgive someone does not mean that you will continue to be in a relationship with them. Some people are too toxic to allow back in your life no matter what. If a person has not acknowledged and changed the wrong behavior for which you have forgiven them, it will likely not be safe to be in a relationship with them. Trust is built upon experience, and forgiveness does not equal trust.

I hope you have found the stories in this chapter to be an encouragement. You also have a story to tell, a highway to travel. No matter where you are in your journey, it is never too late to pick up and begin again. I believe that the harder the life, the higher the calling, and the greater the gifting. We are going somewhere and that somewhere is good! Don't cash in your chips. Keep fighting. Keep believing. Keep going!

CHAPTER FIFTEEN

Spirit and Soul

*"Now may the God of Peace Himself sanctify you through and through; **and may your whole spirit, soul, and body be preserved complete,** without blame at the coming of our Lord Jesus Christ. The One Who calls you is faithful and He will do it."*

1 THESSALONIANS 5:23-24 (NIV, EMPHASIS ADDED)

I n our healing journey it is important to distinguish between the spirit and the soul. As human beings, we are made up of spirit, soul, and body. Our spirit is the part of us that connects with God. I believe that our spirit is made of light, even as God is light. *"God is light and in Him is no darkness at all"* (1 John 1:5, NIV). *"For you were once darkness, but now you are light in the Lord. Walk as children of light"* (Ephesians 5:8). God is called the *"Father of lights"* (James 1:17, NKJV).

Our spirit is designed to be connected to God, to bring forth to both our soul and our body the power, healing, goodness, and love of of God. We are children of God, created to walk on this earth in supernatural activity, even as Jesus did. *"God anointed Jesus of Nazareth with the Holy Spirit and with power, who went about doing good and healing all who were oppressed by the devil, for God was with Him"* (Acts 10:38, NKJV). We were created to be supernatural. It is God's original desire and design for us to function and be alive spiritually—operating in both the natural and supernatural realms. Learning to walk in the supernatural is a process. We grow in our spiritual awareness just as we grow in our natural human understanding and functioning. When Jesus was a boy, He grew in spirit. *"And the Child grew and became strong in spirit, filled with wisdom; and the grace of God was upon Him"* (Luke 2:40, NKJV). We also are invited to grow in spirit and in wisdom.

Our spirit is designed to be in loving leadership over our soul and our body, so that we live in the ever-expanding flow of God's grace and love and healing. We are created to be "super" natural beings! The journey is from being simply natural human beings, to becoming clothed with the light and love of God—*super* natural. Adam and Eve were clothed in the glory of God. When they disobeyed God and ate from the tree of the knowledge of good and evil, the glory departed (so they realized they were naked), and their spirits became separated from the glory of God.

> *Our spirit is designed to be in loving leadership over our soul and our body.*

The glory of God is the radiance of the infinite brilliance and beauty of God. This glory is what was demonstrated when artists painted a halo, a circle of light surrounding Jesus and the saints. As the disciple John said, *"We beheld His glory; the glory of the One and Only who came from the Father"* (John 1:14, NIV).

We are all born into the darkness of fallen human existence, without the covering of God's glory. But God's desire for us is that we receive His "amazing grace" and become a new creation in Him. In this way, we are all on the journey of "re-covery": to be **re-covered in the glory of God**, as His beloved children. This is what the "recovery" process is all about. We were created by God to walk and live covered in His glory! When we receive the life of Jesus into our hearts, we are spiritually born as babes into the Kingdom of God.[1] We receive an awakening in our spirits, an awakening to God, an awakening to that which was lost in the Garden of Eden.

For most of us, our soul (our human nature) is in control. Our soul is our natural personality—our human self—that in us which has the familiar human emotions, thoughts, desires, and behaviors. Our soul also encompasses our difficult emotions and our defenses. It is the part of us that has temper tantrums, that experiences panic, has feelings of being superior or inferior, and can be mean, haughty, aloof, or addicted. Our soul is not designed to be in charge, but to be under the loving leadership of our spirit as our spirit partners with the Holy Spirit of God. When our spirit is in alignment with God, it brings healing to our soul and to our body. Our soul is designed to be brilliant and beautiful as it is led by our spirit. As Psalm 23 (KJV) says, *"He restoreth my soul."*

Several years ago I had an experience of my spirit being in the lead. I had undergone oral surgery and had taken some pain medicine.

I was leaning over the sink that morning, feeling nauseated, and I knew I wasn't going to be able to go to work that day. Spontaneously I prayed "Lord, call my spirit to attention." Immediately I felt fine. I went to work and had a really awesome day! My physical body and my emotions responded to my spirit. When faced with difficult situations I now say, "Lord, call my spirit to attention," or "Lord, let my spirit be awake." Our spirits are designed to have command over our soul, over our bodies. When we allow our spirit to be aligned with God's Holy Spirit, good things result!

It is of utmost importance that our spirit be nurtured if it is to grow, and that our soul learn to yield to the leadership of the spirit! Yielding requires humility and a willingness to change and learn and to be trained. It is not an easy road, especially if you have grown up with rigid authority figures. It is a gradual process of acquiring that great ability to trust.

How do you nurture your spirit? How do you give your spirit opportunities to grow? Here are some ways:

- worship,

- reading the Word of God,

- healthy loving relationships,

- beauty,

- fun,

- music,

- art,

- math,

- ✿ communicating,

- ✿ truth,

- ✿ little children,

- ✿ animals,

- ✿ nature,

- ✿ belonging,

- ✿ adventure,

- ✿ delight,

- ✿ travel.

When I read the Word of God I ask God to let it be my spirit that is reading, not just my soul. Arthur Burk has created a large volume of material on nurturing our spirit (see Appendix). Our spirit is designed to grow in loving relationship with others and with God. We are created to be His family, in love with Him and with each other forever and ever!

1. Special Author Note: In order to be spiritually born into the Kingdom of God, we need to understand that Jesus came into this world to show us who we were created to be: children of God, clothed in glory. He also came to be our Passover sacrifice, so that we could pass over from being spiritually dead to being spiritually alive: *But He was wounded for our transgressions, He was crushed for our iniquities; the punishment that brought us peace was on Him, and by His wounds we are healed"* (Isaiah 53:5, NIV).

We can say, "Lord, thank You for coming to earth as a human being. Thank You for showing me who I really am—a child of God. Thank You for taking the punishment for every sin I've ever committed, every wrong way in which I have walked. I believe in You, that You died for my sins so that I could be holy and whole and filled with Your Spirit of life! Thank You, Abba Father, for not leaving Jesus in the grave, but raising Him up from the dead into eternal life. I receive Your gift of forgiveness, Lord, the gift of eternal life through faith in Your sacrifice of Yourself on the cross. Take up Your true place of authority in my heart. Teach me who You really are, and who I really am. Lead me and let my spirit grow in wisdom and love and every good way that You created me to walk in. Heal my broken heart. Show me the right way to go. Thank You for loving me with a never-ending love. Fill me with Your love and teach me to live 'in love' with You and everyone else. I love You!"

CHAPTER SIXTEEN

Dream Big

When our heart has been wounded and we have reconciled to living a life of quiet desperation as a false self, the dreams of our heart are put into deep freeze. Those dreams need to be rekindled and brought into the daylight. It is so important to dream again. Your dreams are not dead, they have just been waiting for you to let them take flight. It is time now to let yourself dream the big dreams of your heart. No matter how far away or impossible they may feel, your dreams *can* come true. When you recognize that you have a purpose and realize that there is a place for you in this great adventure of life that no one else can fulfill, you can give yourself permission to dream again.

Being real hurts. We have all been bruised. We are all needy. You can acknowledge this, ask for help, and keep asking. Use every difficulty as a stepping stone into glory! You were created for glory, not for pain. The pain is the process to glory. Pain must be acknowledged and dealt with. The deeper the pain, the higher the calling! You are designed for leadership in every area where you have been wounded. Let your hope rise up. There is a purpose in your pain. You are an indispensable player in the game of life. We need you. You have gifts and a part to play that no one else has. You are important and your journey is crucial. The remaining chapters of your life are full of adventure!

So ... what do you want? What do you desire? What excites you and makes you want to dance? Notice, I am not asking what you "should" do or what the right thing is. I'm asking what makes you happy ... what brings you satisfaction and joy? What do *you* want?

Rekindle this exploration of your dreams. What did you like doing as a child? What did you dream about? Who were your heros? Remember times in your life when you felt you were your true self, loving what you were doing. Recapture those times. Dream about what you desire. Journal about this. Talk about it. Google it. Play about it. **Imagine your dreams coming true!** Sing it out! Ask others to tell you what they see as your gifts, what they love about you. There are clues to your destiny all around you. You are on a treasure hunt, a search for the real you. It is time to dream again, and to **DREAM BIG!**

CHAPTER SEVENTEEN

Contending

You desire truth in the inward parts, and in the hidden part
You will make me to know wisdom.

PSALM 51:6 (KJV, PARAPHRASED)

Jacob said to God, "I will not let You go unless you bless me."

GENESIS 32:26 (NLT, PARAPHRASED)

Let us therefore come boldly to the throne of grace, that we may
obtain mercy and find grace to help in time of need.

HEBREWS 4:16 (NKJV)

Jesus said to them, "Do you believe that I am able to do this?"

MATTHEW 9:28 (NKJV)

I believe God wants us to contend with Him for every good thing He has promised us, every treasure that He has built into us, and every dream and desire that we have in our heart of hearts. He does not want us to be satisfied with a humdrum, dull, or desperate life. He has created us to be awesome and beautiful. But ... we must contend for this.

The word contend means to be real. To contend is to argue, confront, be honest, battle, struggle, grapple, push for, dispute, negotiate, wrestle, clash ... hash it out. Whatever it takes, you are not giving up until you are satisfied! To contend means to be emotionally real.

God wants us to express to Him our disappointments, hurts, feelings of abandonment, rage, fear, hopelessness, sadness, confusion, and rejection. He isn't put off by our honesty or offended by our anger and frustration. He wants us to run after Him, tell Him how we really feel, tell Him of our needs, and insist on receiving His help. He does not want us walking on eggshells around Him. Many times we project our relationship with our parents onto God. God does not want us cowering, groveling, scared, or perfectionistic. He is after a real and honest relationship with each and every one of us.

God will never belittle you or ridicule you. God will not condemn you for expressing anger. He does not condemn you for expressing any emotion. He loves you endlessly and He knows what is in your heart. Often, we don't know what is in our own hearts. When we have had overwhelming pain as a little one, that pain becomes suppressed, locked inside (in the "inward parts") and we develop a false self (our "defenses") to live life. But that false self is not the real you. It is just what it says ... false. We can never be satisfied or fulfilled when we live our lives from a false self. And if we live from a false self we can never feel truly loved.

The false self is very strong. To our human understanding, the false self is a kind of savior—saving us from the overwhelming emotions of helplessness, feeling afraid, trapped, hopeless, alone. The false self can be so strong that we don't even know there is anything else to us.

To contend with God means to move beyond the false self, to take responsibility for our own feelings and needs, and to openly and honestly express these to God. However, the false self is *dead set against* this and *never* lets go without a fight! Inside it feels like a life and death struggle to be real and honest and vulnerable. There is a part of us that feels like we will actually die if we get real. Being real and vulnerable with God is what has been described as surrender of

The false self never lets go without a fight!

your life. But it will not happen without contending for it ... with every fiber of your being.

Recently I heard a story from a man (I'll call him Dan) who grew up with a rageaholic, and physically abusive father. Out of all his brothers and sisters, Dan was the one his father picked on the most. In addition to being physically abusive, his father would yell such things as, "Get out of my sight, I don't want to see your face!" Dan and his siblings lived life under the constant fear of "is dad mad?" Dan eventually became a Christian and lived "a good Christian life," doing all the things he supposed God was requiring of him. However, at one point he became ill. He lost his appetite and was very weak. Medical tests found no explanation for his illness. Dan was sick for several years. He could hardly get out of bed and needed help even to get to the bathroom. One night he became very angry (or allowed himself to express his anger) at God.

He said, "I stuck my finger in God's face and shouted (probably among other things) 'You're not doing Your job! You're Word says that You are my healer. Why am I not healed? I've been doing all the right things! Why???!!!" Dan continued saying, "The next morning I woke up hungry for the first time in years." From that time on his health gradually improved and he got better. He asked God, "Why would You finally begin to heal me, only when I unleashed my anger against You?" In reply he felt God was saying, "I was waiting to hear you tell Me how you really felt." Dan had spent years saying, "You are so good," to God, but God doesn't need robots. He wants us to be real with Him.

Often we don't know what we are really thinking inside until we express it in words, either written or spoken. The false self likes to keep us squeaky clean. It so often takes getting to the end of our rope before we are desperate enough to be honest. Sometimes when we allow ourself to be angry, we express our inner beliefs, perhaps for the first time. The only way that we are going to know that God loves us in our painful places is to open up to Him in those spaces.

When the Lord called out to Adam in the Garden, "Where are you?" He already knew where Adam was. He knew that Adam had disobeyed His command and that Adam was hiding. But the Lord intensely desired to have His relationship with Adam restored, and was looking for him to honestly acknowledge what had happened, and to do whatever it would take to come back into the intimate friendship he once had with God. God is *still* calling out to each one of us, "Where are you?" He already knows where we are, but wants us to be honest with Him and come to the place where we believe that He is a good Father and that He loves us.

If life feels boring, dull, monotonous, or desperate, wake your spirit up and cry out to God. Refuse to be content with a safe but unfulfilling life. Find someone who can listen to you and talk to them. Be real. Confront the defenses of your false self. Learn the language of emotions. If what you are doing isn't working, do something else. Put on a new hat. Do something new and uncomfortable. Say what you want! It takes risk to be real. Is it not time to contend for the precious promises of God in your life?

Tools

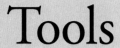

"For we are God's handiwork,
created in Christ Jesus to do good works,
which God prepared in advance for us to do."

PSALM 119:133, NIV

CHAPTER EIGHTEEN

Quieting

One of the greatest indicators of emotional health is the ability to quiet your mind. This is a great challenge, especially if you have suffered a lot of rejection in your life and have not experienced much safety and security in the presence of other people. Be encouraged, the ability to quiet and soothe yourself is a skill—a skill you can learn and develop.

Breathing is a great place to start. Begin by taking a few slow, deep breaths, going slower on the outbreath. When you go slow on the outbreath you enlist your parasympathetic nervous system, which is the part of your nervous system that calms you down. By breathing deeply, you supply lots of oxygen to your brain, which is the opposite of what happens when you are tense.

A good addition to this breathing exercise is to quietly say to yourself on the outbreath:

"Whenever I am afraid, I will trust in You, O Lord"

PSALM 56:3 (CEB, PARAPHRASED)

Though this may sound too simple to actually help, taking three or four slow deep breaths like this can bring your brain into a state of calm.

Print out the following as a reminder:

To Quiet Your Mind

- Take 3 or 4 slow deep breaths, breathing more slowly on the outbreath.

- You may find it helpful to say on the outbreath: "Whenever I am afraid I will Trust in You, O Lord!"

Another great tool for calming yourself is gratitude. Learn to be consciously thankful! Whenever you feel agitated, or even if you just want to feel more peaceful, begin to thank God for things. Train yourself to say things like, "Thank You for my hands, thank You for being able to see, thank You for the beautiful sky, thank You for my shoes …" Anything that comes to your mind, thank Him for it!

Quieting your mind is essential for being able to connect with God. Practice this. You were designed to operate from a quiet and peaceful mind! As Psalm 46:10 (NIV) says *"Be still, and know that I am God."*

I love this Psalm of David:

O Lord, my heart is not proud, nor my eyes haughty; Nor do I involve myself in great matters, Or in thing too difficult for me. Surely I have calmed and quieted my soul; Like a weaned child rests against his mother, My soul is like a weaned child within me. O Israel, hope in the Lord From this time forth and forever.

PSALM 131 (NASB, PARAPHRASED)

Whenever you feel agitated or in need of peace, train yourself to thank God for anything and everything that comes to mind!

CHAPTER NINETEEN

Journaling with Jesus

Most of what I know about journaling with Jesus, I have learned from Mark Virkler. Journaling with Jesus has had such a positive impact on my life. I am excited to share with you what I have learned. Mark teaches about the 4 Keys to Hearing the Voice of God:

- ∾ Quieting your mind

- ∾ Fixing your eyes on Jesus

- ∾ Tuning to the flow of the Spirit

- ∾ Writing the vision

These tools have been extremely important in my life and I use them just about every day. In my work with patients I ask them to look to Jesus. Sometimes this is very difficult to do. If you are avoiding your own heart, it will be hard for you to realize that Jesus is with you. Why? Because <u>He is with you in your heart</u>. Psalm 34:18 (NIV) says, *"The Lord is close to the brokenhearted and saves those who are crushed in spirit."*

Learning to tolerate our pain and learning to trust Jesus to be with us in the very difficult places is a process. We progress in an ever-expanding ability to connect with Jesus and come into His presence. However far you may feel from God right now, be encouraged, we are never too far for God to help. Start wherever you are. Be honest. Tell Him what you are experiencing. It may take time to be able to ask for His help.

It is important to put all this into words. Written words help you to clarify and to become aware of what you are feeling. It is one of the reasons I so strongly recommend journaling. If you don't have an emotional vocabulary, Google a list of emotional words and be as specific as you can about how you feel. Coming to Him, even in a hesitant and unsure way, can open up avenues that you never knew were there!

Don't be in a hurry. Take your time, even if you feel like nothing is going on. I have found that if we spend just a few more seconds with Jesus, something wonderful often happens! We hear something or see something or sense something that changes our perception. Jesus loves to help us.

We hear with our hearts! Even the words "hear" and "heart" suggest this important truth. When our heart has been wounded or crushed, it can be difficult to hear. It is a process and a journey. Taking even a small step in the direction of being real and honest is important.

The first step in journaling is **quieting your mind.** Taking several long deep breaths can be very helpful (see Chapter on Quieting). Or simply do whatever helps you to become quiet inside.

The next step is **fixing your eyes on Jesus**. It is very important to visualize. Habakkuk 2:1 (NIV) says, *"I will look to see what He will say to me."* It doesn't say "I will <u>listen</u> to <u>hear,</u>" but "I will <u>look</u> to <u>see</u> what He will say to me." This is crucial. We look to God in order to hear Him. The ability to visualize—to imagine—is a gateway into the realm of the spirit. Pictures are the language of the spirit.

So, after quieting your mind, imagine yourself being with Jesus - sitting together or perhaps walking on a beach. Focus on the visual— how Jesus *looks* to you. You might imagine holding His hand or looking into His eyes.

As you visualize yourself with Jesus, begin to talk with Him. You may have written down a question you want to ask Him, or you can write down the things that you are thankful for. You can ask "What do You want me to know right now, Lord?" Notice the thoughts which may come bubbling up as you continue to look to Him. The voice of God is often expressed in spontaneous thoughts. Sometimes the things that God is saying to you may sound just like your own thoughts. Do not judge what you are hearing at the time, simply write it down. Respond with your heart to what you sense the Lord is saying to you. Write down your responses. Writing the words will help to focus your attention. As an added benefit, because you wrote them down you will be able to retrieve these thoughts for reflection later on.

After you have *quieted your mind* and *fixed your eyes on Jesus,* the next step in the process is **tuning into the flow of the Spirit.** If you start to judge what you are hearing, you may switch from your heart to your head and break the flow of the exchange. Tuning to the flow of the Spirit has to do with staying in an open-hearted posture, soft and attentive to what you are seeing and hearing. Later you can judge whether what you have heard seems to have truly been from the Lord.

The final step in the journaling process is to **write the vision!** Writing down your questions, Jesus' responses, and then your responses to what He has said is a vital part of the journaling process. You can continue this process for as long as you choose. Habakkuk 2:2 (NKJV) says, *"Write the vision, make it plain on tablets (your journal), so he (you) may run (move forward) who reads it."* Putting your thoughts and revelations into words will greatly facilitate the process of understanding yourself and receiving God's love and guidance for your journey.

One way to assess this is to ask yourself, "Does what I have heard agree with the Word of God? Also, as you begin this process, and even when you become experienced at it, it is often helpful to receive input from others. This is especially necessary if you have been journaling about making any type of major decision. Ask someone you trust, someone who has maturity in hearing from the Lord, to review your journaling with you and give you feedback about it's accuracy. Psalm 15:22 (NKJV) tells us that our plans will be established with the help of *"a multitude of counselors."*

Above all else, seek the Lord. Above all else, seek the Lord. He promised us that if we seek Him with all of our heart, we will find Him (Jeremiah 29:13, NIV, paraphrased). This is a process and a journey. If you are not in this place right now, that's okay. Don't let the idea overwhelm you and keep you from giving this a try. Do what you can do, and follow the flow of your own heart.

Many times when I feel down or discouraged, I simply turn my eyes to Jesus and journal for a few minutes. The effect this has on me always amazes me. What I hear from Him encourages me and sets my feet back on the path of life.

Journaling with Jesus is a wonderful way to get to know Him and yourself. You can journal on any topic—nothing is off limits! Write down your questions, your goals, your daily schedule, your ideas about your purpose in life, your relationships, your physical health … you can journal your questions about Scripture, asking God for understanding. You can ask Jesus about anything!

> *"Call to Me, and I will answer you, and show you great and mighty things, which you do not know."*
>
> JEREMIAH 33:3 (NKJV)

CHAPTER TWENTY

Capacity

Capacity is the ability to tolerate and feel emotions. It can be learned only in the presence of others who can help you develop this skill. We are designed to be able to tolerate our painful emotions and to return to joy in about 90 seconds, at around age two. What a child needs is a mother who knows how to do this and can help them do it too! For most of us, this is an ability that we learn later, as an adult, during the healing process.

In order to develop capacity, we need to be able to experience our deep and scary feelings in the presence of a safe person. You cannot do this by yourself. We need to learn how to put words to our feelings so we can understand what the feelings are and know that they are normal. We need to hear from another person that they have had similar feelings, that they understand, that they have learned how to handle their feelings, and are able to come back to feeling good again. Eye contact is very important. When your brain can "see" that

We are born imitators, and we need healthy people to imitate.

another person is with you and can tolerate what seems so overwhelming, your brain learns that you can do this too. We are born imitators, and we need healthy people to imitate. Healthy people help us learn the way back from being alone with wretched feelings.

Some of the words we use to describe our difficult emotions are: scared, afraid, trapped, helpless, overwhelmed, alone, abandoned, terrified, angry, hurt, rejected, ashamed, guilty, hopeless, devastated, unsure, embarrassed. It is important to get as specific as you can in describing your feelings. For example, the word "uncomfortable" or "upset" is a good place to start, but if you can be more specific, it will help you really share your heart with the person you are learning to trust. In the chapter, *Feel to Heal*, we learned that we are created to feel and to heal, and that this is not only possible, but it is a big part of the pathway to your purpose in life!

I learned from Dr. Jim Wilder that in order to build capacity to tolerate painful emotions, it is necessary to first build our capacity for joy! As Dr. Wilder defines it, joy comes from being with people who are glad to be with you. The more joy you have experienced, the more you can tolerate painful feelings. So maximize your time with people who understand you and love you and enjoy you!

CHAPTER TWENTY-ONE

Food

Food is a vital part of the healing process. When a child is wounded, whether it's abandonment or abuse, food is often the only comfort they can turn to. Many times a child will bond to food instead of to people. This is a malfunction of the way we were created to connect. The kinds of foods that a hurting child will become addicted to are usually foods that bring a "high"—a sense of euphoria. Unfortunately foods that create this euphoric feeling are unhealthy foods which hit the brain quickly. Having perhaps little experience with healthy balanced relationships and stable emotions, a suffering child will try to avoid feeling overwhelmed and devastated by ingesting something that will bring a feeling of elation. Thus begins the pattern of great lows and great highs. The brain learns that certain foods can catapult us out of the overwhelming negative feelings and make us feel really good. The process of addiction is the same, whether the substance is heroine or Hershey's® chocolates. This pattern of turning to addictive foods is emotionally crippling and interferes with the ability to actually deal with and process feelings so that a person can grow and heal. You cannot go backward and forward at the same time!

It's interesting that the foods a child finds comforting and addictive, things like sugary sweets, bread, ice cream, dairy products, etc., are often the foods many of us become allergic to as adults. Some have called it allergic/addicted. If there are foods that you crave (this applies to alcohol as well) it is likely that that food is causing a chemical reaction in your body which is actually blocking your brain's ability to process emotional pain. That food may very well be causing you to feel good or high, but may actually be contributing to emotional instability. These same foods we crave often produce inflammation throughout the body, causing chronic pain, and contributing to a multitude of medical problems including arthritis, cancer, diabetes, high blood pressure, heart disease, and much more.[1]

Certain foods may be causing you to feel good or high, but may actually be bringing emotional instability.

People who really want to heal and become all that they can be are those who, little by little, get a handle on what they are eating and drinking. There are foods we have grown up eating that are just plain not good for us. They will bring your energy level down, cause brain fog, and create emotional ups and downs. These include:

- sugar,

- foods made with sugar,

- white anything (bread, pasta, rice—anything white has been processed so that the minerals and vitamins that should be there aren't, and they will leech those nutrients from your cells),

- processed and artificial foods,

- unhealthy oils, and

- meats that have been treated with antibiotics and hormones.

The most healthy foods are raw, organic vegetables and low glycemic fruits. Lean organic meats and nuts provide a good source of protein which is stabilizing to the blood. It's not what you eat 10% of the time, it's what you eat 90% of the time that will keep you moving in the right direction.

Changing your eating habits is a challenge. It is a process which takes time and attention. Without healthy bodies, we can't do much on this planet. I encourage you to take it slow, to begin reading on this subject, and then gently begin to change self-destructive eating patterns. Because so many people are involved in the pursuit of a healthy lifestyle, there's a ton of information out there. Ask for help in this area. Get guidance and support. Don't become a fanatic, just become a student of good health. Your body will greatly appreciate it! Nurturing the health of your physical body will strengthen you greatly in your quest for emotional healing and becoming all that you can be ... Bon appetit!

Endnote:

1. www.savvypatient.com

CHAPTER TWENTY-TWO

Play

"You can discover more about a person in an hour of play than in a year of conversation."

PLATO

"Men do not quit playing because they grow old; they grow old because they quit playing."

OLIVER WENDELL HOLMES JR.

"Play is the highest form of research."

ALBERT EINSTEIN

"Play is often talked about as if it were
a relief from serious learning. But for
children, play is serious learning."

MR. ROGERS

"Unless you are converted and become as little children,
you will by no means enter the kingdom of heaven."

JESUS (MATTHEW 18:3, NKJV)

Play means to express yourself in a real way, authentically and without filters. Play requires honesty. It can't happen without openness and being yourself, uninhibited. Connected from the heart, not the head. Play is about freedom to be—to explore … in the moment. When you play you are alive to what is and what the possibilities are. You are awake to learn and discover. So … take some risks! Try new things. Do something different. Put your toes in the water, or maybe just jump right in. Pretend. Make believe. Imagine!

Okay, now you get the idea. Try it! Take 15 minutes here and there and allow yourself to play. Just give yourself permission. Tell that little boy or little girl inside your heart that they have 15 minutes to play anything they want. Let your heart decide what to play.

So, this is what just happened. As I was going over the editing of this chapter, I said to myself, "Hey, that's a really good idea," so I decided to allow myself to have 15 minutes to play (it turned into a half hour). I had a really neat time—exceptional in fact. I made a great discovery and I talked to my neighbor who I've been meaning to talk to for about a month (but was too scared). It was fun and very different from my usual way of being. By the way, the only adult I know who really plays like this is Jim Goll. Check him out!

If that word "play" seems scary or stupid to you, understand that this is coming from the point of view of the false self. The false self wants to be in control, to wear the correct mask to make sure it is accepted by others. Play lets the real you out of the box. This threatens the image the false self has worked so hard to project. So there can be a rather intense struggle to be real!

Play lets the real you out of the box.

Allowing yourself to play can help you in every way. Play lets you to have more fun, feel better physically, make new discoveries, and even be more creative and productive at your work. If you are doing what you love to do, your work can become like play. And that is where the finances start to flow! When you are doing what you love to do, what you were created to do, and enjoying it, your creative juices gush forth and you draw to yourself all the resources that you need to be awesome!

So tiptoe out of your usual routine … and spend some time playing! If you are fortunate enough to have a little child with you, they can help you get the hang of it. But even if you don't, give it your best shot anyway. Your inner child will love it.

CHAPTER TWENTY-THREE

Words of Life

Here are some words from the Bible that have meant a great deal
to me in my work with the healing of emotions. These truths
point the way to our Creator's plan for restoring our broken hearts.
God is not unaware of our brokenness. He has a path and a plan for
us which includes healing and restoration, wholeness, and the joy of
healthy relationships!

There are many ways you can use these words. One way is to
ponder them. You might choose one each day and meditate upon it
throughout the day, much like having a snack that you can nibble on
as you go about your business. You might write them down in your
journal and ask any questions that come up for you. You can also
draw or doodle in your journal whatever comes to you about these
words. You can read them out loud with your own name inserted and
make them personal for you. This is great because they <u>are</u> meant

personally for you! You can put them to song. These words are for you, to bring life and joy and hope. I bless you to receive all the nourishment that God intended for you through these words.

"When my father and my mother forsake me, the Lord will adopt me as His child."

PSALM 27:10 (AMP)

"Come to me, all you who are weary and burdened, and I will give you rest ... for I am gentle and humble in heart, and you will find rest for your souls."

MATTHEW 11:28-29 (NIV)

"Trust in Him at all times, you people; pour out your hearts to Him, for God is our refuge."

PSALM 62:8 (NIV)

"Do not fear, for I have redeemed you; I have called you by name; you are Mine! When you pass through the waters, I will be with you; And through the rivers, they will not overflow you. When you walk through the fire, you will not be scorched, nor will the flame burn you. For I am the Lord your God, the Holy One of Israel, your Savior ..."

ISAIAH 43:1-3 (NASB)

"He (God) Himself has said, 'I will never leave you nor forsake you.'"

HEBREWS 13:5 (NKJV)

"The Lord is near to the brokenhearted and saves those who are crushed in spirit."

PSALM 34:18 (NIV)

"Many waters cannot quench love, nor will the rivers overflow it."

SONG OF SONGS 8:7 (NASB)

"Behold, You desire truth in the inward parts, and in the hidden part You will make me to know wisdom."

PSALM 51:6 (NKJV)

While Jesus was here on earth, he offered prayers and pleadings, with a loud cry and tears, to the one who could rescue him from death. And God heard his prayers because of his deep reverence for God. Even though Jesus was God's Son, he learned obedience from the things he suffered.

HEBREWS 5:7-8 (NLT)

"He will cover me with His feathers, and under His wings I will trust."

PSALM 91:4 (KJV, PARAPHRASED)

"Nothing can separate me from the Love of God which is in Christ Jesus our Lord."

ROMANS 8:39 (NIV, PARAPHRASED)

"Jesus said, 'Did I not tell you that if you believe, you will see the glory of God?'"

JOHN 11:40 (NIV)

Trust in the Lord with all your heart, And lean not on your own understanding; In all your ways acknowledge Him, And He shall direct your paths.

PROVERBS 3:5-6 (NKJV)

"Love never fails."

1 CORINTHIANS 13:8 (NKJV)

"He shall feed His flock like a shepherd: He shall gather the lambs with His arm, and carry them in His bosom, and shall gently lead those that are with young."

ISAIAH 40:11 (KJV)

"I will not leave you as orphans; I will come to you."

JOHN 14:18 (NIV)

"… you have received the spirit of adoption by whom we cry out, 'Abba, Father.'"

ROMANS 8:15 (NASB, PARAPHRASED)

"Your gentleness makes me great."

PSALM 18:35 (NASB)

"I will give you the treasures of darkness and hidden riches of secret places."

ISAIAH 45:3 (NKJV)

(Jesus said) I will do what the Father requires of me, so that the world will know that I love the Father.

JOHN 14:31 (NLT)

"My God will supply all your needs according to His riches in glory in Christ Jesus."

PHILLIPIANS 4:19 (NASB)

"'For I know the plans I have for you,' declares the Lord, 'plans to prosper you and not to harm you, plans to give you hope and a future.'"

JEREMIAH 29:11 (NIV)

"Call to Me and I will answer you, and I will tell you great and mighty things, which you do not know."

JEREMIAH 33:3 (NKJV)

O Lord, my heart is not proud, nor my eyes haughty; Nor do I involve myself in great matters, Or in things too difficult for me. Surely I have composed and quieted my soul; Like a weaned child rests against his mother, My soul is like a weaned child within me.

PSALM 131:1-2 (NASB)

"For we are God's handiwork, created in Christ Jesus to do good works, which God prepared in advance for us to do."

EPHESIANS 2:10 (NIV)

"And we know that in all things God works for the good of those who love Him, who have been called according to His purpose."

ROMANS 8:28 (NIV)

"See what love the Father has given us, that we should be called children of God!"

1 JOHN 3:1 (RSV)

"If we confess our sins, He is faithful and just to forgive us our sins and to cleanse us from all unrighteousness."

1 JOHN 1:9 (NKJV)

Cast all your cares on Him, for He cares for you.

1 PETER 5:7 (RSV, PARAPHRASED)

"… with everlasting kindness I will have mercy on you."

ISAIAH 54:8 (NKJV)

"I have loved you with an everlasting love."

JEREMIAH 31:3 (NKJV)

"The Lord is my shepherd; I shall not want. He makes me to lie down in green pastures; He leads me beside the still waters. He restores my soul; He leads me in the paths of righteousness For His name's sake. Yea, though I walk through the valley of the shadow of death, I will fear no evil; For You are with me; Your rod and Your staff, they comfort me. You prepare a table before me in the presence of my enemies; You anoint my head with oil; My cup runs over. Surely goodness and mercy shall follow me all the days of my life; and I will dwell in the house of the Lord forever."

PSALM 23 (NKJV)

CHAPTER TWENTY-FOUR

More Useful Tools

There are a lot of ways to help yourself while you are on the road to recovery. Here are some suggestions:

- **Stimulate both sides of your brain.** Doing anything that is bilateral will help your brain to process emotions by stimulating both sides of the brain. My favorite is walking, but canoeing, running, dancing, tapping your hands alternately, or any other alternating right/left activity will help your brain to process emotional material.

- **Color.** Coloring is a tool that can help you express your emotions. You can do this in a number of ways. One is to simply get a big sheet of paper, some crayons and just color. (I'm not talking about using a coloring book here, I suggest you to have a blank canvas so you can freely express what is inside of you.) Another is to purposely color what you are feeling and then to add a few words to it as the meaning of your feelings becomes clearer to you. Allow yourself to be creative! (The false self may think this is stupid, but persevere!) Coloring will help you to focus on, express, and become more aware of what you are feeling and why. You can also simply draw a picture, which is another good way to express whatever is inside. Showing your coloring or drawing to a trusted counselor or friend may shed further light on your process.

∽ **Doodle.** Doodling is another way to access your real self. Simply let yourself make doodles, they don't need to look like anything. Add a word here or there for punctuation. Whatever comes to you, let yourself express this onto the paper.

∽ **Journal.** Simple journaling is another tool. This is being honest about your emotions in words. Allow yourself to have different points of view. Journal your internal dialogue, the things you say to yourself in your head that you never express out loud to others. <u>The ultimate goal is to know and love yourself.</u> Journaling helps the internal conflicts become clear so that you can make decisions based on understanding yourself.

I have found that it is just about impossible for some people to journal. If this is true for you, then what can help is to find a counselor or friend who you can trust, and begin to use spoken words to express the real needs of your heart. As you become more comfortable with emotional honesty, you may develop the ability to journal your feelings and desires.

᜖ **Talk to someone.** This may seem obvious, but talking about your struggles and emotions is very important. Telling your story to someone who can listen will greatly help to facilitate the healing process. The person who is on the listening end need only listen and encourage you to express yourself. They should not try to fix or change you, but simply listen.

᜖ **Take your feelings seriously.** It is important to not be afraid of intense emotions. It is only when you are emotional that your beliefs can change. Both the right and left sides of your brain must be engaged for change to occur. If you stay "in your head" (left brain active, meaning thinking/analyzing, which is often a defensive posture) your true beliefs will be unavailable for modifying. Notice when you are escaping from what is in your heart and make a determination that you are going to be real and honest about how you feel.

᜖ **Eat better.** Eating healthy foods will give you the physical stamina to be able to process your emotions. Sugar is a mood altering substance, as is any other food to which you are addicted. Often the foods you crave are the ones which create havoc in your body. Healthier choices when eating are a mainstay for emotional healing.

᜖ **Do Math.** Working math problems is a good way of helping yourself to feel better when you are overwhelmed. Math brings you into the left side of your brain which is the logical side, and away from the right side, which is the emotional side. Try it!

‰ **Exercise.** Exercise improves your mood. Not only does it can provide bilateral brain stimulation, but aerobic exercise also helps the blood to remain alkaline, which makes for a healthy brain.

‰ **Practice Centering Prayer.** Several years ago a man sitting next to me on an airplane first demonstrated and then told me about Centering Prayer. I have used it ever since, and it's been a mainstay of my spiritual journey. In Centering Prayer you sit quietly and open up your heart to God. You choose a "sacred word" and allow it to be gently present. Whenever you become aware of distractions, gently return to the Lord with the use of your sacred word. Do this for 20 minutes and then allow whatever prayer is in your heart to come gently into words.

‰ **Do something new!** *Anything* new will be a challenge and will help you to learn more about yourself. Be willing to change and step out of old patterns!

‰ **Cultivate joyful relationships!** Joy comes from another person or persons being glad to be with you. Joy builds the capacity of the brain to tolerate painful emotions. So, be with people who love you and enjoy you! Limit your time with people who are continually down and out. Especially if your goal has been to help them or fix them. And stay away from people who are chronically angry, which is toxic. Pets can also be tremendously nurturing. Seeing a tail wag excitedly when you come home can make you feel welcome and loved; stroking a furry friend can calm stress and relax you; playing lets your mind step into the moment; being nuzzled or cuddling a pet can be wonderful ways to feel emotional warmth and share joy.

- **Be grateful.** Being thankful is an important skill. Thankfulness actually simulates joy in the brain. If you begin to notice things for which you can be thankful, and then speak aloud what you are thankful for, it can change your mental state quickly.

- **Sing.** Little snippets of positive songs can be a great way to encourage yourself.

- **Spruce yourself up.** Get some new and attractive outfits. Pick clothes that fit you well. Get rid of your dumpy old clothes. Have your makeup done professionally. Try a new hairstyle. Get a massage or a facial. Be good to your physical body!

- **Pay attention to your dreams while sleeping.** Dreams often reflect emotional reactions we're having that we are not aware of. Dreams are messages to you to help you understand where you are in life and where your purpose is leading you. Dreams can show you things you are doing that are positive or not so positive. They can also show you the progress you are making and lead to ideas that will benefit your recovery process. I encourage you to keep a journal by your bedside and to write down your dreams. Telling your dreams to others also facilitates understanding. Ask God for healing dreams and also for help in understanding your dreams!

- **Limit negative media.** People who have experienced a lot of fear in their life will sometimes be addicted to dark drama, horror shows, or even to the news. This is called being fear-bonded. We need to break the fear bonds, and create love bonds through healthy relationships. People who are angry will sometimes gravitate toward angry music. This does not facilitate the healing process, but is more likely to further bond you to fear and negativity. Begin to wean yourself from negative media, and find someone with whom you can talk over your feelings.

* **Read.** Read biographies of people who have gone through difficult circumstances and have learned and grown from their experiences. You can absorb a lot from someone else's story. Read stories that focus on the recovery, not the trauma. If you look through the Amazon Customer Reviews you can get an idea of which books will be the most valuable to you.

* **Go outdoors.** Being outside in nature is a great way to self-nurture. Take off your shoes and wiggle your toes in the grass or in a stream. Drink in the soothing colors of the earth and sky. If you are home-bound or can't get out, look at pictures of nature in books or on the internet. Don't let what you can't do stop you from doing what you can do!

* **Make a list of the promises of God to you in the Bible.** They are many and they are awesome. Recite these to yourself out loud on a regular basis, especially in times when you need encouragement. This helps to build your spirit and nurture your "true self" in the image of God.

* **Ask God for help!** Ask and keep asking. Ask for what you need. Ask to be led in the right direction. Ask for healing. Ask for protection and security. Ask for help in understanding what you are going through. Ask to be encouraged. Ask for

joy! Ask for favor. Ask to receive every extravagant gift that your Creator wants to give you!

CHAPTER TWENTY-FIVE

Jokes

"A merry heart does good, like a medicine ..."

PROVERBS 17:22A (NKJV)

I love jokes! So I thought I would include some in this book. If things get rough with reading about the traumas and woundedness, you can dip into some jokes for relief. The following are some of my favorites, but I encourage you to figure out what tickles your funny bone and keep a handy supply!

- How many psychiatrists does it take to change a light bulb? Only one, but the light bulb really has to want to change!

- Did you hear about the new restaurant on Mars? The food is out of this world ... but there's no atmosphere!

- The psychiatrist was trying to engage the family's cooperation in changing the belief system of her patient, who believed he was a chicken. But one of the family members piped up and said, "But doc, we really need the eggs!"

- What do you call a chicken who runs back and forth across the road and then jumps into a puddle of mud? A dirty, double-crosser.

- A policeman pulled over a man who had a group of penguins in the back of his truck. The man hesitated when he was asked where he got the penguins, so the officer said, "Look, buddy, I want you to take those penguins to the zoo right now, got it?" The next day, don't you know it, the policeman saw the same guy with the penguins still in the back of his truck. "Hey buddy," the officer said, "Didn't I tell you to take those penguins to the zoo?" "Oh yes, officer," he said. "Yesterday we went to the zoo, and today we are going to the museum!"

- This man was overweight and had a lot of health issues, but would not take his wife's advice to eat healthy. Finally, he had a heart attack. His doctor told him that if he wanted to stay alive, he was going to have to change his diet. Reluctantly he agreed. He and his wife became exemplary health food fans. They lived another 20 years or so. Then the wife died, and shortly afterward her husband died. When he got to the pearly gates St. Peter welcomed him in, showed him his mansion, and then asked if he would like to see the banqueting hall. As his wife joined him, they entered a huge and beautiful dining hall, tables loaded with all kinds of rich foods and tantalizing desserts. The man turned to his wife and said, "Honey, I can't eat any of this stuff, it's not on my diet." "Oh no," St. Peter said, "there are no calories here, you can eat anything you want and it won't hurt you!" The man turned to his wife and said, "We could have been here 20 years ago!"

∞ A Priest, a Minister and a Rabbi were discussing how they use the collection money that they get during their services. The Priest said, "We draw a line on the ground, and then we take what we've received in the collection and throw it up in the air. Whatever falls on the right side we give to God, and whatever falls on the left, we take for ourselves." The Minister said that his church does something similar. "We draw a circle on the ground, throw the collection up in the air, and whatever comes down inside the circle, they give to God, and the rest they keep for themselves. The Rabbi said, "We have an even better method: we simply throw the collection up in the air. We figure that whatever God wants He'll take and whatever comes back down we keep!"

∞ What happens when a duck flies upside down? He quacks up!

CHAPTER TWENTY-FIVE

Summing Up

Thank you for taking this journey with me. We have talked about many aspects of the healing process and the courage it takes to awaken to your real self. This book holds a tremendous amount of material—much of which has taken me the better part of my lifetime to understand. We have discussed the wounds that all of us human beings sustain. We've examined the importance of being honest, of putting words to our feelings, of finding safe people to help us, and of moving through the pain into the joy of being our true selves and being able to love others from a pure and innocent heart.

We have talked about God's love for us and His desire to heal us, as well as the challenge of learning to trust Him on our journey. We've discussed the difference between our spirit and our soul, and have noted the importance of having our spirit lead and our soul becoming beautiful as it follows. We have considered the idea that in the places where we are wounded, those are the places where we are gifted to bless and encourage others. We have recounted several stories of people who have come through the healing process in some area of their lives.

I now bless and encourage you to go forth with courage on your journey, to use the tools that seem to fit for you, and to earnestly desire the highest and the best for your life. No matter how dismal and discouraging your circumstances may be right now, no matter how many mistakes you have made, no matter what anyone else has said about you, your life is important. You are a child of God. Your heavenly Father created you because He loves you and wants you to know what real love is—the kind of love you dreamed about as a little one.

I bless you with knowing you have all that you need within you, and I bless you with the holy and healing relationships that you will need as you grow. There is no end to the potential that is yours.

With all my heart,

Susan M. Austin, MD

Appendix

"... I will strengthen you, I will help you,
I will uphold you ..."

ISAIAH 41:10, ESV

APPENDIX A

Declarations

Declarations are a powerful and positive way to direct your mind and bring encouragement to your soul. A useful way to use these declarations is to say out loud, "I call my spirit to attention," and then to proclaim the declarations with great spirit-led enthusiasm! You can also make copies of these pages and carry them with you.

I declare, in the Name of Jesus Christ of Nazareth:

That my spirit is awake to God and His purposes for me!

I am special, unique, and precious to God.

God is working in me always to bring me to the fulfillment of my destiny. His plans for me are good!

God has a good and satisfying work for me to do! I delight to do His Will.

Through His Son, Jesus Christ, I am alive to God and dead to sin!

God's Love is in me, casting out fear at all times!

I agree with God's Love. I agree with God's Truth.

I am filled with God's Goodness and Grace.

Every difficult thing in my life is working out for good, and I trust God to accomplish this.

I use every difficulty as a stepping-stone into Glory!

I was created to carry the Glory of God!

Everything about me is designed to be a vessel of God's Being!

I do not shrink back from hardship, but I awaken more and more to the purposes of God for me. I lean on Jesus for all that I need!

I look for, notice, and celebrate God's fingerprints in my life!

I am thankful in all things.

My life is hidden with Christ in God! I belong to Him and to His Family! Hallelujah! Amen!

Here is another declaration which we wrote together in my women's group:

Lord, I thank You that You are orchestrating the changes in my life. I trust You in this.

Bring me the change I need. I can change. I am able to change. I have the capacity to change.

I can always tell You how I am feeling even when I am very scared, and You are faithful to give me courage.

I will not walk in fear, but declare that God is with me, and is leading me.

When You say, "Go," I will go, and when You say, "Stop," I will rest.

You keep me on my path. You give me assurance.

The discomfort of change assures me that I am alive, and that I am becoming and moving toward all that God has placed within me of His giftings and inheritance.

I will lean on God who desires good for me, and look to Him to direct my paths, even though I don't know where I am going.

I reach out to You for Your love. Lord, work in me.

Yay, God!

Spirit Blessings

You can read these blessings out loud to yourself to nurture your spirit, or to another person to nurture their spirit. If you are reading this to another person, it is best to speak out their name, for example: "Mary, precious child of God, I call your spirit to attention …" (You do not have to be with the person to speak this blessing to them. You can speak to their spirit from another room, or even from another city or country!)

Precious child of God, I call your spirit to attention. I call your spirit to hear that you are a beautiful and beloved child of God.

As the Word of God tells us in 1 John 3:1 (ICB), *"The Father has loved us so much! He loved us so much that we are called children of God. And we really are his children!"*

Child, your heavenly Father loves and cherishes you. He is with you always, guiding you, drawing you with His lovingkindness, caring about the smallest details of your life. For He loves you with an everlasting love and is calling to you with His lovingkindness (Jeremiah 31:3, NKJV paraphrase).

You are important to Him and valuable, just because you are you. Your heavenly Father's value of you is not dependent upon your performance. He loves and cherishes you simply because you are you—His very own child. There is nothing you can do to make Him love you more, and there is nothing you can do to make Him love you less. You are His precious creation, a unique reflection of who He is, created for your own special good works that no one else is capable of.

As we hear from Romans 8:17 (NIV), *"Now if we are children, then we are heirs—heirs of God and co-heirs with Christ."* Precious child, God your Father has created you to be an heir to His Kingdom, to live in the beauty and abundance of a loving relationship with Him and with everyone else in the Kingdom! You are His special and unique creation. You are gifted in ways and combinations like no other creation of His.

I bless you with revelation of the specific and unique person that you were created to be. I bless your eyes to see and your ears to hear, to find the clues which are all around you, clues to your particular and special destiny and purpose. I bless you with expectation of good in your future. I bless you with a sense of great adventure as you look toward who you are and the excellence that God has placed in you.

As we hear in 2 Timothy 1:7 (NKJV), *"God has not given you a spirit of fear, but of power and love and a sound mind."* Spirit, child of God, you have received power to accomplish all that you were created to be and do! You have the indwelling love of God within you, that love which overcomes. That love which is a fountain of blessing for all of your friends. That love which never fails is already within you.

It matters not what things look like in the present. Even as we see a baby as unable to do much of anything, we know that given time and care, that child will be able to walk, to read, to do so many things that are not apparent in infancy. And you too, spirit, have within you the potential that God placed there. The seeds of life are within you, and your times are in His hands. His love can accomplish all that He has designed for you, as you partner with Him in the outworking of His excellent plan for your life. You are a beautiful creation of God. As the Word of God says in Isaiah 41:10 (NLT), *"Don't be afraid, for I am with you. Don't be discouraged, for I am your God. I will strengthen you and help you. I will hold you up with my victorious right hand."*

God has set the specific time of your birth and the exact family that He designed for you to be born into. God had you in His heart and mind before the world was created. From Acts 17:26-28 (KJV paraphrase) we hear: *"God has made everyone on earth, and has determined beforehand when we would live and where we would live, so that we should seek the Lord, in the hope that we might search for Him and find Him, though He is not far from each one of us; for in Him we live and move and have our being ..."* We are His offspring.

Child of God, I bless you to rest in the understanding that you have within you the potential for greatness and joy and all that your heart desires! Your Creator has designed you for greatness! *"Fear not, little flock, for it is the Father's good pleasure to give you the Kingdom"* (Luke 12:32, KJV).

Spirit, I bless you to be awake, to awaken more and more to the purposes for which you were created. I bless you with childlike faith, to explore, to be curious, to dream, to imagine, and to savor all that has to do with your purpose and destiny. Your heavenly Father has perfect timing for the outworking of His plans for your life. His plans for you are good and will satisfy your deepest desires. I bless you to receive revelation of who you are in your Heavenly Father's eyes and to enjoy the dream for you that has been in His heart forever.

Here is another blessing for your spirit:

Dear child of God, I call your spirit to attention. You are a treasure and a blessing. There is no one else like you. You have been created by God for a special purpose in this world, a purpose that no one else can fill. You are God's child and He is watching over you in the outworking of His plan for your life. Everything in your life is designed to draw you to Him, to help you to know Him and trust Him—the amazing beauty of the earth as well as the difficult times when you need someone to depend on and to help you.

Spirit, child of God, the Lord wants to be your all in all. He wants you to know Him as a loving Father, perhaps quite unlike the experiences you had with your earthly father.

He is patient and kind with you. He is confident in what He has placed in you and confident of His ability to bring you forth into the glorious plan He has for your life. You are created to be more than human. Just as Jesus was more than human, so you are created to tap into the resources of God and to "walk on the water" with Him! You are made in the image of God and are designed to carry His Glory! And guess what? It is all by faith! Your faith is your ability to see beyond the merely human point of view and to access the supplies of God's Kingdom.

There is a Bible verse from Luke 12:32 (NKJV) which says *"Do not be afraid, little flock, for it is your Father's good pleasure to give you the Kingdom."* This is a great secret and a great mystery, but you are created to be God's child! You are created to receive all that you need from the tender hand of your loving Creator and Father. Over and over, Jesus tells us to not be afraid, but to trust Him and to trust God. What seems impossible for human beings is not impossible for God.

So, rise up in your heart, child of the Holy One! You are beautiful and you are beloved. You have everything you need to step forth into the life that God has created you for. Get ready for a great adventure. Begin to see yourself as beloved and special! Open the eyes of your heart more and more to the goodness which surrounds you. Let your heart be soft and open. And talk to God, the loving Father who created you. He longs to hear your voice and to gently parent you in all the ways that you need to learn and grow.

There is a Book of Adventures with your name on it. You are the heroine of your story. So step beyond the fear and begin to imagine the life that you have always wanted. If your heart is in your dream, no request is too extreme. I bless your heart to know that you are loved and cherished, special and unique, gifted and equipped. It is time to receive all that you need and to imagine, just imagine what it will be like to have your dreams come true!

Here is another spirit blessing:

Beloved child of God, I call your spirit to attention. I call your spirit to gently hear that you are precious and dearly cherished by your heavenly Father who created you. I bless you to hear that you are incredibly gifted as God's own child. You have talents and abilities that go far beyond what the mind of your soul can imagine.

The Bible states in 1 Corinthians 2:9-10 (NKJV): *"Eye has not seen, nor ear heard, nor has it entered into the heart of man the things which God has prepared for those who love Him. But God has revealed them to us through His Spirit."* You, spirit, are the part of your being that is able to connect with the Spirit of God. For, *"He who is joined to the Lord is one spirit with Him"* (1 Corinthians 6:17, NKJV).

Spirit, I bless you to know that you are one Spirit with the Holy Spirit of God, inseparable, made of the same light that God is. Spirit, child of God, I bless your eyes to see and your ears to hear and your heart to receive the full ongoing revelation of who you are as God's precious child, and all that He has in store for you. For you are designed by your Creator to carry the Glory of God. The Glory of God, His radiance, His beauty, His wisdom, His kindness, His comfort and love, His healing, His provision … all of this is your birthright as His treasured child. It is through your faith that you receive His Glory and dwell in this beautiful Glory of God. There is nothing you can do to earn the Glory of God. It is a free gift, secured for you by the death and resurrection of your precious Savior, Jesus Christ.

I bless you, spirit, to exercise your faith to believe, to receive, and to rest in God's sweet promises for you. As you dwell in the Secret Place of the Most High, which is His Glory, by faith and rest, you receive His protection, comfort, healing and blessing. All that you need is found in the Glory of God. Philipians 4:19 (NASB) says, *"My God will supply all your needs according to His riches in Glory in Christ Jesus."* Ask and you will receive. Ask and keep asking. Look and keep looking. I bless your eyes to see and your heart to believe in the riches of His Glory!

Every difficulty you encounter is meant to be a stepping stone into the Glory of God, if only you will believe that He is with you, that He loves you, that He is able to help you in your time of need. Spirit, I bless the faith that is in you to look to the Lord in every difficult situation. I bless your eyes of faith. For Christ is in you, the hope of Glory! (Colossians 1:27, NKJV paraphrased). *"In Him we live and move and have our being"* (Acts 17:28, KJV). *"Lift up your heads, O ye gates! And be lifted up, you everlasting doors! And the King of Glory will come in. Who is this King of Glory? The Lord strong and mighty, The Lord mighty in battle. He is the King of Glory!"* (Psalm 24:7-8, 10).

He is with you always, child of God. I bless the faith that is within you to see and comprehend and receive all that you need. Isaiah 60:1-3 (NIV) says, *"Arise, shine, for your light has come, and the Glory of the Lord is risen upon you. See, darkness covers the earth and thick darkness is over the peoples, but the Lord will arise upon you and his Glory will be seen upon you. Nations will come to your light, and kings to the brightness of your rising."* Spirit, child of God, you are created to carry the Glory of God in this world as we declare *"Let the whole earth be filled with His Glory!"* (Psalm 72:19, NKJV).

With God, nothing is impossible, and so shall it be for you as you trust in Him, rest in Him, and look to His Glory for all of your needs. Spirit, child of God, I bless you with the blessing of Ephesians 1:17-19 (NASB) *"That the God of our Lord Jesus Christ, the Father of Glory, may give to you a spirit of wisdom and of revelation in the knowledge of Him. I pray that the eyes of your heart may be enlightened, so that you will know what is the hope of His calling, what are the riches of the Glory of His inheritance in the saints, and what is the surpassing greatness of His power toward us who believe."*

Spirit, child of God, I bless you to rest and trust and look to Jesus and rejoice in the great outworking of His good plan in your life, one that will fill your heart with joy unspeakable and full of Glory!

APPENDIX C

Journaling with Jesus

In the Tools section of the book, I provided a chapter on Journaling with Jesus. If you have never journaled or feel uncomfortable about how to begin, I invite you to re-read chapter 19 (page 113) now. Below please find some quick and easy steps to help guide you as you journal.

Find a quiet place where you can relax and be alone with Jesus. Before you begin to journal, write our your concerns or a question.

1. Quiet your mind (take a few slow deep breaths).

2. Fix your mind on Jesus (imagine being with Him). Focus on what you are seeing.

3. Tune to the Flow of the Spirit and ask your question.

4. Write what you are seeing or hearing.

Do not judge what you are hearing or feeling, just write it down— you can evaluate it later.

For more help with journaling: www.cwgministries.org

APPENDIX D

To Do List

☐ Take responsibility for yourself—for your feelings and needs.

☐ Spend quiet time with yourself.

☐ Turn toward your feelings, and be honest.

☐ Ask God to help you.

☐ Determine that you are going to love yourself.

☐ Put your feelings and thoughts into words, written or spoken.

☐ Admit that you need help.

☐ Spend time with people who love you.

☐ Take time to play.

☐ Journal.

☐ Write down your dreams. Think about them and talk about them.

☐ Practice thankfulness.

- ❏ Read over and over God's promises to you.

- ❏ Laugh a lot.

- ❏ Be in nature as much as you can.

- ❏ Face your fears.

- ❏ Read up on healthy food and eat healthy.

- ❏ Exercise.

- ❏ Be gentle and patient with yourself.

- ❏ Ask yourself what you want in every area of your life.

- ❏ Then go toward those things.

- ❏ Be honest with God.

- ❏ Nurture your spirit.

- ❏ Take your time in the healing process.

APPENDIX E

Coming Out
of Hiding

Here is a picture that I drew several years ago, depicting the little abandoned real self beginning to come out of hiding, to be real. The inscription reads:

**"You little one
too scared to move,
I see you
so small
and bleak,
weak,
trembling.**

**How is it that you
are still alive?**

I'm so glad you are."

APPENDIX F

To a Friend

I would like to dedicate this poem, which I love, to all the many people who have helped me and encouraged me on my path, and in the writing of this book.

You entered my life in a casual way,
And saw at a glance what I needed;
There were others who passed me or met me each day,
But never a one of them heeded.

Perhaps you were thinking of other folks more,
Or chance simply seemed to decree it,
I know there were many such chances before,
But the others—well, they didn't see it.

You said just the thing that I wished you would say,
And you made me believe that you meant it;
I held up my head in the old gallant way,
And resolved you should never repent it.

There are times when encouragement means such a lot,
And a word is enough to convey it;
There were others who could have, as easy as not,
But, just the same, they didn't say it.

There may have been someone who could have done more
To help me along, though I doubt it;
What I needed was cheering, and always before
They had let me plod onward without it.

You helped to refashion the dream of my heart,
And made me turn eagerly to it;
There were others who might have (I question that part)—
But, after all, they didn't do it.

GRACE STRICKER DAWSON

APPENDIX G

The Promises of God

The following are some of the biblical promises of God to us, His children. I encourage you to read them out loud and put your own name in them. These are especially helpful to read over during times when you are feeling small and insignificant.

"For I know the plans I have for you," declares the LORD, "plans to prosper you and not to harm you, plans to give you hope and a future."

JEREMIAH 29:11 (NIV)

The Lord is my Shepherd, I shall want for nothing. He makes me lie down in green pastures, He leads me beside the still waters, He restores my soul.

PSALM 23:1-3 (NKJV)

God is our refuge and strength, a very present help in trouble.

PSALM 46:1 (NKJV)

Do not be afraid, for I am with you; do not be discouraged, for I am your God. I will strengthen you; I will help you; I will uphold you with my righteous right hand.

ISAIAH 41:10 (NIV, PARAPHRASED)

And my God will supply all your needs according to His riches in glory in Christ Jesus.

PHILIPPIANS 4:19 (NASB)

When my father and my mother abandon me, the Lord will take care of me.

PSALM 27:10 (NLT, PARAPHRASED)

And God is able to make all grace abound to you, so that you always have everything you need, that you may have an abundance for every good deed.

2 CORINTHIANS 9:8 (NKJV, PARAPHRASED)

I will never leave you or forsake you.

HEBREWS 13:5 (RSV)

His divine power has given us everything we need for life and godliness through our knowledge of Him who called us by His own glory and goodness. Through these He has given us His very great and precious promises, so that through them you may participate in the divine nature and escape the corruption in the world caused by evil desires.

2 PETER 1:3-4 (NIV/NKJV COMBINED)

I am with you always, even to the end of the age.

MATTHEW 28:20 (NKJV)

The righteous cry out, and the Lord hears them; He delivers them from all their troubles. The Lord is close to the brokenhearted and saves those who are crushed in spirit.

PSALM 34: 17-18 (NIV)

He who has begun a good work in you will complete it.

PHILIPPIANS 1:6 (NKJV)

Ask, and it will be given to you; seek, and you will find; knock, and it will be opened to you. For everyone who asks receives, and he who seeks finds, and to him who knocks it will be opened.

MATTHEW 7:7-8 (NKJV)

God causes all things to work together for good to those who love God, to those who are called according to His purpose.

ROMANS 8:28 (NASB)

But they that wait upon the Lord shall renew their strength; they shall mount up with wings as eagles; they shall run, and not be weary; and they shall walk, and not faint.

ISAIAH 40:31 (NKJV)

Call to me and I will answer you and tell you great and unsearchable things you do not know.

JEREMIAH 33:3 (NKJV)

There is a river whose streams shall make glad the city of God, The holy place of the tabernacle of the Most High (that's us).

PSALM 46:4 (NKJV, PARENTHESIS ADDED)

"Then you will call upon me and come and pray to me, and I will hear you. You will seek me and find me; when you seek me with all your heart, I will be found by you," says the LORD.

JEREMIAH 29:12-14 (RSV)

Nothing ... will be able to separate us from the love of God which is in Christ Jesus our Lord.

ROMANS 8:39 (NIV, PARAPHRASED)

"Fear not, for I have redeemed you; I have called you by your name; you are Mine. When you pass through the waters, I will be with you; and through the rivers, they shall not overflow you. When you walk through the fire, you shall not be burned, Nor shall the flame scorch you. For I am the Lord your God, The Holy One of Israel, your Savior.

ISAIAH 43:1-3 (NKJV)

We who have believed enter into rest.

HEBREWS 4:3 (KJV, PARAPHRASED)

Praise the Lord, my soul, and forget not all his benefits—who forgives all your sins and heals all your diseases, who redeems your life from the pit and crowns you with love and compassion, who satisfies your desires with good things so that your youth is renewed like the eagle's.

PSALM 103: 2-5 (NIV)

APPENDIX H

Trustworthy Tidbits

You are likely to recognize many of these sayings. They are well known and so widely spread that I am unable to credit most of their original authors. Several are things I have jotted down while reading or listening to my favorite speakers, while others are popular sayings I have adapted along the way. They are so poignant and have been so helpful to me that they are worth sharing with you. I invite you to enjoy them and make them your own!

- You are a one-of-a-kind creative genius!

- The greatest predictor of lifelong mental health is the ability to quiet your mind.

- If you have one foot on the gas, and one foot on the brake, the brake wins.

- The darkest time is just before the dawn.

- Be kind, because everyone you meet is in a great battle.

- As with the crucifixion, sometimes victory does not look like victory.

- If you don't give yourself attention, you'll try to get it from others.

- The greater the pain, the higher the calling and gifts.

- What kept you safe as a child, often keeps you stuck as an adult.

- You cannot solve an internal problem with an external solution.

- When the "good" part of yourself can begin to accept and embrace the "bad" part (that which you don't like about yourself), healing happens.

- You can only take one little step at a time.

- Garbage in, garbage out.

- You were created to solve problems.

- Making mistakes is healthy—it's how we learn and grow!

- The deeper sorrow has carved into your being, the more joy you can contain.

- You cannot go backward and forward at the same time.

- Forgiveness is not the same as trust.

- Only when our emotions are engaged can our beliefs change.

- Every difficult thing in your life is Father-filtered, and will pan out for your good.

- You can only go as fast as your slowest part.

- It is often very uncomfortable to make healthy decisions.

- Nothing is impossible with God.

- Run toward your giant!

- Your gifts and talents will often come out of the places of your deepest pain and insecurities.

- The ability to ask yourself how you are doing is an important skill.

- If you are going through hell, keep going.

- Don't let what you can't do stop you from doing what you can.

- All you ever really have is now.

- If you look with the eyes of your heart you won't see the wrinkles.

- Follow your passion.

- Love never fails!

APPENDIX I

Going Deeper

Suggested Reading List

- *A Grace Disguised* by Gerald Sittser

- *Awakening the Slumbering Spirit* by John and Paula Sandford and Lee Bowman

- *Blessing Your Spirit* by Arthur Burk and Sylvia Gunter

- *Bo's Café* by John Lynch and Bill Thrall

- *Codependency: Love and Codependency—How To Improve Communication and Love Yourself In A Codependent Relationship* by Erica Harding and Cody Dean

- *Counseled by God: Emotional wholeness through hearing God's voice* by Mark and Patti Virkler

- *Faith That Hurts, Faith That Heals/Understanding the Fine Line Between Healthy Faith and Spiritual Abuse* by Stephen Arterburn and Jack Felton

- *Freedom from the Religious Spirit* by C. Peter Wagner and Chuck Pierce

- *4 Keys to Hearing God's Voice* by Mark Virkler

- *Healing Life's Deepest Hurts* by Edward M. Smith

- *Hearing God: For Intimacy, Healing, Creativity, Meditation, and Dream Interpretation* by Dr. Mark Virkler and Patti Virkler

- *I Was Busy, Now I'm Not* by Joseph Peck, MD

- *Joy Starts Here* by E. James Wilder and Edward M. Khouri

- *Jumpstart* by David Herzog

- *Left to Tell: Discovering God Amidst the Rwandan Holocaust* by Immaculee Ilibagiza

- *Parenting From the Inside Out* by Daniel J. Siegel MD and Mary Hartzell

- *Search For the Real Self* by James Masterson

- *The Christian Codependence Recovery Workbook* by Stephanie Tucker

- *The Complete Guide to Living With Men* by E. James Wilder

- *The Divided Mind* by John Sarno MD

- *The Healing Touch of God* by Agnes Sanford

- *The Life Model: Living From the Heart that Jesus Gave You* by James G. Friesen and E. James Wilder

- *The Mystery of Spiritual Sensitivity* by Carol A. Brown
- *The Sacred Romance* by John Eldredge
- *Understanding the Wounded Heart* by Marcus Warner
- *Waking Up In Heaven* by Crystal McVea and Alex Tresniowski

Suggested CDs

- *Developing Your Spirit* by Arthur Burk
- *Ministering to Babies in the Womb* by Arthur Burk
- *Nurturing Your Spirit* by Arthur Burk

Suggested Websites

- www.inward-bound-adventures.net
- www.joystartshere.com
- www.savvypatient.com

Dr. Susan is available to come to your community for speaking engagements (large groups) or seminars (smaller groups of 10 – 30). She teaches on many aspects of emotional healing, and specializes in leading group experiences utilizing creative exercises and practical tools for growth and becoming all you were created to be!

To learn more, to invite Susan to speak or conduct a seminar, or to attend an Inward Bound Seminar or Webinar please visit:

www.inward-bound-adventures.net

www.couragetobereal.com